Beyond The Shadows:

A Theology of Suffering and Hope

By: John R. Kuykendall

Beyond The Shadows: A Theology of Suffering and Hope
Copyright © 2025 Redeeming Family Press
Published by Redeeming Family Press
Grand Rapids, MI

All Rights Reserved. No part of this book may be reproduced, stored in retrieval services or used in any manner without the prior written permission of the publisher except for the use of brief quotations in a book review.

Scripture quotations are from the King James Version Public Domain

Hardback ISBN 979-8-9914491-5-1

Dedication

To the wonderful saints of Pilgrim's Rest Baptist Church who by patient perseverance show the world what it means to love Jesus and suffer for His glory. Watching your lives made writing this book a labor of love.

Remembering without ceasing your work of faith, and labor of love, and patience of hope in our Lord Jesus Christ, in the sight of God and our Father. 1 Thessalonians 1:3

Table of Contents

Introduction..7

1. Pain Desires An Answer...............................9

2. The Sovereignty of God.............................23

3. Suffering Through The Crucible................37

4. Suffering Through Phyiscal Ailments.......51

5. The Response of Faith..............................67

6. Does Jesus Care?......................................80

7. The Prayer of Faith...................................96

8. No More Tears...107

Bibliography...124

6

Introduction

Christians disagree on a host of issues, one of which includes suffering. How we think about, process, respond to, and live in light of suffering will differ depending on our understanding of God's Word. This became most evident to me when I had conversations with a dear friend. He is godly, sincere, and earnest in his faith and I rejoice in the grace of God so evident in his life. He and I began to consider the role of suffering in the believer's life. As we discussed these issues it occurred to me that I have spent very little time in my ministry helping those entrusted to my care develop a theology of suffering. I soon became convinced I needed to teach a series on the subject. As I made plans to teach a theology of suffering, I felt compelled to turn the series of messages into a book. I needed to give God's people scriptural answers for their suffering. This book is intended to encourage those called to suffer. For those, such as my friend mentioned above, who may read this book, I pray the words contained herein will be received in love from one desiring to strengthen the body of Christ.

This book does present some arguments in favor of my particular theological position regarding suffering as it is not possible to write a book of this sort without making theological arguments. I pray that those who are suffering can gain valuable and practical insights into their suffering. If we do theology properly it should lead us into an understanding of what we are to do with the truths presented. That is, theology is not merely theoretical and academic, it is practical. Theology teaches us how to live before the face of God. I pray this book helps you reach a better understanding of God's purposes in allowing suffering and how we as Christians ought to think regarding the sufferings of this life. May God bless you as you read these words and may God bless my feeble attempt to strengthen His people.

1
Pain Desires an Answer

For I reckon that the sufferings of this present time are not worthy to be compared with the glory which shall be revealed in us. Romans 8:18

Do we as Christians speak about suffering too much, or not enough? Do we have a thoroughly biblical understanding of suffering? At a pastor's fellowship I attended many years ago, a very kind, gracious, and biblically grounded pastor named Roger was asked to bring the first message of the day. I do not remember his text, and I must confess I don't remember a lot of what he said. However, I distinctly remember Pastor Roger describing times of difficulty in which God made His presence known. The Pastor, whom my mother thought the world of, also testified of God's faithfulness amid challenges experienced by the Church he was pastoring. I appreciated the message even though as a young man I knew very little about suffering.

The next pastor who was asked to speak went out of his way to tell us he wouldn't be talking about hard times or troubles. In his words, "We hear too much about it." If he uttered that unnecessarily pointed phrase once, he uttered it ten times over the course of his message. That is all I remember of his message. That and his unkempt appearance. Was this sloppy and somewhat combative pastor right? Do we hear too much about suffering?

We may hear and talk a lot about suffering, but are these conversations informed by the Bible? Are our convictions and beliefs rooted in the truth of God's word, or something else? It is incumbent on pastors especially, who all ought to be theologians, to drive this conversation so that we may help people come to see the trials, the most mundane things of life, and the most horrendous suffering through the perfect lens of Scripture. But this isn't just the duty of pastors and theologians. The layperson must also develop a biblical understanding of suffering. Not only for the trials of life that will inevitably come but also for those whom the Lord will allow you to minister to.

We all ought to desire to glorify God in every area of life. Solomon reminds us in the book of Ecclesiastes that God has placed eternity into man's heart. We must see things with an eternal perspective. Too often our conversations regarding suffering are dominated by subjective thought, sentimentality, and a focus on the temporal. I pray our discussion here will help encourage all of us to consider the theology of suffering.

Someone may still ask why we need a theology of suffering. Is it helpful to focus on suffering? There is indeed a real danger of developing an unhealthy fixation on suffering. We have all known people who see trouble coming down every road. These people, as my wonderful mother-in-law observed, borrow trouble. The danger of an unhealthy fixation on something does not diminish the need to view the truth accurately. A corrected biblical view of suffering may unburden those who borrow trouble! In these chapters, I will show the necessity of a theology of suffering through a thoroughly biblical and experiential study.

What Is Suffering?

It is necessary here to answer two basic questions regarding suffering. Specifically, we need to establish what suffering is and from where it originates. In one sense it may not be necessary to define suffering. We all know what suffering is and are at least vaguely familiar with the concept even if our lives are untouched by suffering. Nevertheless, words and concepts have meaning and we can't accurately discuss a thing if we don't know exactly what it is. For us to grow in a Godly perspective on suffering, we need to know God's perspective, and we need to know the boundaries and essential realities of suffering.

Elizabeth Elliot aptly defined suffering as, "having what you don't want or wanting what you don't have" (Elliot, 2019). That seems to be a succinct definition. None of us want sickness. None of us wants to lose a loved one. We don't want rejection, poverty, persecution, physical pain, or trouble of any kind. Conversely, there are things we do want but do not always have. We do want comfort in life which includes health, a comfortable home, the joy of friends and family, sufficient money to pay bills, and to be left alone to pursue the things we love. Not everyone has those things. We are often plagued with things we don't want and are left destitute of things we sincerely want.

"Man that is born of a woman is of few days, and full of trouble. He cometh forth like a flower, and is cut down: he fleeth also as a shadow, and continueth not." Job 14:1-2

Where Does Suffering Originate?

Suffering is ultimatley the result of sin. All suffering comes as an immediate, delayed, intended, or unintended consequence of sin. That doesn't mean suffering is always the direct result of our sin. As we will see later on in chapters three and four, Scripture is filled with examples of those who were right with God, not living in open sin yet they suffered. The point here is that suffering is ultimately traced back to the garden when man fell in his sin.

Suffering always has a connected relationship with sin. Whether that is our own sin, the sin of Adam in the garden, or someone's sin between then and now. Suffering comes as a result of sin. God promised Adam life and happiness so long as he obeyed. Man was placed in paradise and given every good thing by his creator. This creature from the dust was given a single prohibition to not eat of the tree of the knowledge of good and evil (Genesis 2:17). By implication, life and happiness were promised if Adam continued in obedience. Death was the curse associated with disobedience. Despite the perfection of the joys of this perfect paradise, man obeyed his lust rather than God and fell from his original state. The curses associated with the fall were imposed by God.

"Death and the forces of wear and erosion operate in our universe in accordance with the sentence pronounced upon mankind- 'Dust thou art, and unto dust shalt thou return.' The special favor of God's co-ordinating (sic) hand no longer guarantees perfection and order in life or the uninhibited growth of crops and fruits. A tendency to chaos and disorder has invaded all nature so that men must sweat to clear the

thorns and thistles of the field for their food and survival."
Masters, 1998, 2013

Many would argue that sickness and suffering always come from Satan, but it was God himself who withdrew the blessings of Eden. Satan tempted, but it was God in fulfillment of his Word, who brought consequences on all those involved in the sin of Genesis 3. Furthermore, I do not think it can be demonstrated that Satan can cause sickness or even death. The sovereign King of the universe holds absolute power over these things. Suffering then is the result of sin. God is sovereign over us and has a purpose in our suffering. We will see this truth in more detail in chapters two and three.

Scripture Gives Us A Theology Of Suffering

As I have indicated, Pastor theologians must teach the truths contained in God's Word. The truths regarding any given concept are not often spelled out in their entirety in any single portion of Scripture. For example, not everything the Bible says about the Holy Trinity may be found in a single chapter or verse. God has gifted His Church with men who can systematize these truths so they can be taught to us.

We also have confessions of faith that accurately summarize the truths of scripture. As a Baptist Pastor, I'm thankful that these confessions of faith from previous generations are available to help guide our conversations. When conversing with someone who asks "What do Baptists believe?" We can show them the 1689 Confession of Faith or the Baptist Faith and Message 2000. These documents provide a succinct statement of our beliefs, guidance, and help protect us from error. Similarly, godly men have given the Church volumes on systematic theology to help us understand the truths of God's word. The same must be true, although perhaps to a lesser extent on the truths regarding suffering. We are right to spend time and energy learning how to think about the fundamental truths of our faith. In the same way, we should learn to think properly about the suffering of this present time. We do well in seeking to gain an eternal perspective of our suffering. Scripture gives us this perspective. Give attention to the words of the Apostle Paul recorded in Romans 8:18-23.

> *"For I reckon that the sufferings of this present time are not worthy to be compared with the glory which shall be revealed in us. For the earnest expectation of the creature waiteth for the manifestation of the sons of God. For the creature was made subject to vanity, not willingly, but because of him who hath subjected the same in hope, Because the creature itself also shall be delivered from the bondage of corruption into the glorious liberty of the children of God. For we know that the whole creation groaneth and travaileth in pain together until now. And not only they but ourselves also, which have the firstfruits of the Spirit, even we ourselves groan within ourselves, waiting for the adoption, to wit, the redemption of our body." Romans 8:18-23*

Time and space will not permit a full exposition of this passage, but a few helpful observations will be made. The apostle, Paul, assumes the reality of suffering in this text. Paul does not attempt to prove suffering as a concept, rather he asserts that suffering is a reality in this present life. His original readers needed no proof of the reality of suffering. The early church was well acquainted with poverty, sickness, persecution, and sorrow of all varieties. In 1 Corinthians 4:11-13, Paul describes the suffering he and many others were subjected to.

> *"Even unto this present hour we both hunger, and thirst, and are naked, and are buffeted, and have no certain dwelling place; And labour, working with our own hands: being reviled, we bless; being persecuted, we suffer it: Being defamed, we intreat: we are made as the filth of the world, and are the offscouring of all things unto this day."*
> 1 Corinthians 4:11-13

We are thousands of years removed from the context in which Paul was writing, yet we have no difficulty grasping the truth he details. In 2025, God's people still know what it means to suffer. Paul's words in Romans 8 provide a boundary for the sufferings of life. He calls them the "sufferings of this present time." As my pastor often says, "It won't always be like it's always been." The sufferings you and I experience as God's people are limited to this brief time we spend on earth. One day, Christ will make all things new. We read in Revelation that there will be a new Heaven and a new earth (Revelation 21). The former things of life will be gone on that day. We long for that day when our God will fold the present reality like a garment and make all things new. Indeed, as Paul said, the entire creation groans and travails until that day. For now, we rest in the everlasting arms of Him who works all things after the counsel of His own will.

> *"In whom also we have obtained an inheritance, being predestinated according to the purpose of him who worketh all things after the counsel of his own will: That we should be to the praise of his glory, who first trusted in Christ." Ephesians 1:11-12*

Suffering Is A Reality

My mother would often say, "It's nice to talk about the sweet by and by, but we live in the nasty now and now." Perhaps that was her paraphrase of Romans 8. Suffering is a reality in our world. Scripture is filled with examples of suffering. Abel, the first person mentioned in the great hall of faith in Hebrews 11 suffered. Abraham was not exempt from suffering. Moses willingly chose to suffer affliction with God's people rather than be known as the son of Pharaoh's daughter. We have already mentioned Job, but he rightly understood his suffering came from the hand of God. Joseph told his brothers in Genesis that God meant his suffering for good. The prophets of the Old Testament were well acquainted with grief. Jesus himself suffered physically and not just on the cross. Jesus prepared His disciples for trouble when he said,

> *"Verily, verily, I say unto you, The servant is not greater than his lord; neither he that is sent greater than he that sent him." John 13:16*

If our Lord suffered, so will we. The disciples did indeed suffer greatly as did the early Church.

Even if we had no knowledge of Scripture, we would understand the reality of suffering. History gives us a record of human suffering. The Black Death is estimated to have taken the lives of somewhere between 75 and 200 million people across Europe, Asia, and Africa during the 14th century. Wars in recent history such as World War 2, and Vietnam have claimed thousands of lives. Even today, wars fought around the world are tragic reminders of suffering. Just recently, hurricanes Helene and Milton left devastation and loss of property and life in their wake. Not all of history is blotted with tragedies like the black death, but war, poverty, sickness, infant mortality, and other forms of suffering have been the rule throughout history and not the exception.

Our own experiences inform our understanding of suffering in this world. As I write this section, my mind's eye scans the congregation of Pilgrim's Rest Baptist Church, and as I do, I am quickly reminded of the reality of suffering. Empty seats remind us of those who have suffered and some who suffer illness even now. Some in our family have had children die in infancy. Others have had children suffer childhood diseases and die young. Some have had children who joyfully fight through various physical difficulties. Some have experienced devastating physical injuries. Few in our small congregation have been exempt from the sufferings of this present time. This wonderful body of believers, if given the option, would no doubt choose to escape these things, yet the hand of God is clearly seen in their sorrow and I can confidently say that with Paul, they rejoice in tribulation.

My mother, who died in 2002, at the age of 51, fought cancer for years before her death. Not only did she fight cancer, but she and my dad fought desperately to care for my younger brother who is severely autistic. They both wanted desperately to care for him at home, but the more he grew the more difficult it became even with help provided. Ultimately, they had to put him into a home. The difficulty of this decision was compounded by the disapproving sneer and ostracization of some who did not attempt to understand or show grace. Was all this suffering for naught? I assure you it was not. God was at work then as He is now. God's people suffer and God has a wise and holy purpose in allowing our sorrow. The purpose of God in suffering will be explored later.

Pastor Roger, the kind pastor I mentioned at the beginning, suffered physically for years before he died. You probably have similar stories in your memory of people who suffered. Greg Ogden, in his book Discipleship Essentials (Ogden, 2007), tells the story of Jerry Sitser. Jerry was traveling in his van with his wife, mother, and four Children in 1991 when a drunk driver swerved into his vehicle, changing his life forever. In an instant, Jerry lost his wife, mother, and young daughter. Most of us will never experience pain like this and cannot imagine how we would cope. Jerry struggled for a time but eventually learned to trust God even with this massive tragedy he did not understand. As Ogden explains,

> *"Jerry Sitser will go to the grave without knowing the full meaning of the loss of his family, but in the years since this tragedy, time is bringing perspective to Jerry, and the good from the tragedy is starting to emerge." Ogden, 2007*

Time would fail us to give more examples, but we see the vivid reminders of suffering daily, and many of these reminders are etched in our memories forever.

Enemies of Christ

Those who oppose Christ and His Word have a theology of suffering, therefore we must learn to think biblically about suffering. We must know how to answer the Atheist (one who denies the existence of God), the Apostate (one who has left the faith and now opposes it), as well as the purveyors of false religion. Atheism is not new and the Bible has long endured skeptics who rage against it. The arguments raised against God's existence are not new either. One of the oldest arguments against God is the problem of evil. Modern proponents of new Atheism will often cite the problem of evil in their arguments. Those who Apostatize from the faith will often cite evil as a leading reason for their rejection of the faith. The argument has been variously articulated from ancient to modern Atheists.

Epicurious, the ancient Greek philosopher, famously put forth this alleged dilemma when he asked, "Is God willing to prevent evil, but not able? Then he is not omnipotent. Is he able, but not willing? Then he is malevolent. Is he both able and willing? Then whence cometh evil? Is he neither able nor willing? Then why call him God?" (Bishop, 2016). The dilemma has been variously answered and though it may appear formidable, the answer is not as difficult as it would seem. The Scriptural argument for the problem of evil will be addressed later in our study, but the answer is that God is sovereign. It should also be noted that some of Epicurus's presuppositions are false.

Free will is another answer given when discussing the enemies of Christ. After all, God doesn't want robots right? This answer may be appealing but is entirely inadequate. If we say suffering is a reality because of man's free will, we are partly right, but it does not provide a sufficient answer to the objector. Christ possessed a free will yet was without sin. Was Christ a robot? Of course not. So then, it is possible to be free and holy. Furthermore, when God's people are all gathered together in heaven, it is generally understood that we will have free will. I have not heard or read anyone argue otherwise. If we will have free will in Heaven how can it be promised that sin, sorrow, and suffering will not be present? Will we all be robots in Heaven? No! The question may sound absurd, but it is a fair question if free will is the answer to the problem of evil. Furthermore, Scripture provides accounts of God preventing evil without violating the will of the creature. As we see, freedom is possible with the absence of evil.

Since the enemies of Christ use the problem of evil as an argument against God, we all must be prepared to provide an answer. Some are more gifted than others, but the idea that apologetics and evangelism are only for a select few is a pernicious error.

> *"But sanctify the Lord God in your hearts: and be ready always to give an answer to every man that asketh you a reason of the hope that is in you with meekness and fear." 1 Peter 3:15*

Parents, and Grandparents, your children must be equipped with these answers. If you hope to have these answers provided to them through a few hours in Church each week, and tragically often less, you are sadly mistaken. How do we give our children these answers? The Word must be in the very fabric of who we are. It must be a topic of discussion that is as natural as commenting on the weather.

> *"And these words, which I command thee this day, shall be in thine heart: And thou shalt teach them diligently unto thy children, and shalt talk of them when thou sittest in thine house, and when thou walkest by the way, and when thou liest down, and when thou risest up. And thou shalt bind them for a sign upon thine hand, and they shall be as frontlets between thine eye." Deuteronomy 6:6-8*

The Abuse of Scripture

My comments on this point will be brief, but it is important to state that it is a grievous error to suppose God's people should never suffer. It is often argued that God's people are promised health. When we are sick we need only pray in faith for healing and if we pray in faith we will always have healing. It is further argued that sickness always comes from Satan. Neither of these propositions can be substantiated with clear Biblical teaching. It is no wonder that prosperity preachers do not preach expositionally. You show me a church that teaches the prosperity gospel and I will show you a church that shuns expository preaching.

Prominent teachers like Joel Osteen, Benny Hinn, Creflo Dollar, Keneth Copeland, Joyce Meyer, Jesse Duplantis, and countless others propagate the idea that being a Christian means God wants you to be healthy, and prosperous all your life. The ideas put forth by many of these teachers are more pagan than Christian. Speaking success and health into your life as many encourage sounds more like an incantation than Christian theology. Many sincere believers are duped by this erroneous doctrine and countless others see the error but are not equipped to answer. May God strengthen His church to understand, believe, and defend His truth.

I hope by now at least a few things are clear. Suffering is a reality. God's people suffer, and amid this suffering, we do not despair for we know our God is sovereign in all things and is accomplishing His glory and our good through the trials of life. May God enable us to trust Him always regardless of what we may experience.

"Now the God of hope fill you with all joy and peace in believing, that ye may abound in hope, through the power of the Holy Ghost."
Romans 15:13

2
The Sovereignty of God

"The counsel of the LORD standeth forever, the thoughts of his heart to all generations." Psalm 33:11

Why do bad things happen to good people? This is the question many experiencing suffering ask. It is sometimes said, referencing Jesus, "That only happened once, and He volunteered for it." Though a bit snarky the answer is theologically correct. But that answer doesn't satisfy the aching heart searching for answers in the midst of suffering. Nor does this theologically correct answer show much Christ-like compassion. The answer to this question lies in an understanding of God's sovereignty. Suffering is a reality because God allows it. At first, that may not sound comforting but I pray all who read this learn the joy of resting in the God whose counsel stands forever. The God we serve has the hairs of our head numbered (Luke 12:7) and is working all things out for our good and His glory. (Romans 8:28)

The problem of evil, as this topic has been historically called, is perhaps one of the most common objections to Christianity. Those who are not Christians will use the reality of suffering as grounds to refute God's character as being one that is good. It has now become a trend for those who deconstruct their faith. Too often the attempts to answer these questions of suffering and the character of God seek to get God "off the hook" or worse, apologize for Him. God does not need a defense. He isn't on trial. Humanity is not judge over the Almighty God. The Sovereign King (creator) of the universe does not need us (His creation) to apologize on His behalf.

Certain foolish people have stated that God will owe them an explanation when they stand before Him on judgment day. Such a statement is the height of folly. These individuals have a tragically inflated view of self, and a terribly undervalued view of God Scripture describes the dread of those who stand before the One to whom we must all give account. John describes this terrible scene in the Book of Revelation.

> *"And I saw a great white throne, and him that sat on it, from whose face the earth and the heaven fled away; and there was found no place for them. And I saw the dead, small and great, stand before God, and the books were opened: and another book was opened, which is the book of life: and the dead were judged out of those things which were written in the books, according to their works." Revelation 20:11-12*

God is not on trial and He will not answer to the demands of those who would join Satan in seeking to dethrone Him. Abraham rightly recognized God as judge of all the earth in Genesis 18:25. Just as Abraham bowed to the God who as sovereign creator has the wisdom and authority to judge His creatures, so must we. We have failed to follow His commands. We leave off what we ought to do, and do those things we ought not. Not a single one of us would be able to stand before His righteous judgment on our own. He is the judge of all the earth and no one receives injustice at His hands. This does not mean our God is aloof and unwilling to provide answers. Indeed He has given His Word which is sufficient to answer our questions if we will humble ourselves before Him. Let us now consider free will, the problem of evil, and the comforting reality of God's sovereignty for those who suffer.

As we previously observed, many well-meaning Christians will point to free will as the answer to why bad things happen. Though this is partially true, it cannot be the entire answer. I once overheard two ladies discussing the tragedy that took place in New York on September 11, 2001. In responding to why God would allow such a tragedy, one of the ladies exclaimed, "God had nothing to do with that!" Was she right? Was God merely a bystander like the rest of us? Was God as helpless as those of us who were fixated on the television in horror and bewilderment? Does the omnipotence of God end where the choice of the creature begins? Even beyond examples of tragic evil that humans inflict on other humans, What about sickness, death, poverty, persecution, and other forms of suffering? Does God's sovereignty only extend so far? Is He powerless as His creation suffers under the weight of a sin-cursed world exacerbated by the attacks of Satan? Is Satan to blame for all suffering? Can such a view be maintained from Scripture that God is a bystander during all our suffering?

I submit that such a view cannot be maintained based on the Bible. All of these questions have answers found ultimately in the sovereignty of God. God is sovereign and He has a purpose in suffering. We will discuss His purposes later, but for now, we will focus on the proposition that God is sovereign. If we are to understand suffering we must first understand that God is sovereign. This means that all things are under His watchful care. Nothing happens to us that is not under His watchful and loving eye. Even in suffering, we can be assured that our God is on the throne and His intentions for us are good and holy. Now unto the King eternal, immortal, invisible, the only wise God, be honor and glory forever and ever. Amen (1 Timothy 1:17).

The Epicurus Dilemma

"I am the LORD, and there is none else, there is no God beside me: I girded thee, though thou hast not known me: That they may know from the rising of the sun, and from the west, that there is none beside me. I am the LORD, and there is none else. I form the light, and create darkness: I make peace, and create evil: I the LORD do all these things."
Isaiah 45:5-7

We have already touched on the Epicurus dilemma in the previous chapter, but I want to briefly highlight it again before we move on to the answer to the problem of evil, the sovereignty of God. For the sake of review, here is the dilemma attributed to Epicurus and argued by skeptics and atheists throughout history.

> *"Is God willing to prevent evil, but not able? Then he is not omnipotent. Is he able, but not willing? Then he is malevolent. Is he both able and willing? Then whence cometh evil? Is he neither able nor willing? Then why call him God?"*
> Bishop, 2016

Many atheists use some form of the Epicurus dilemma to disprove God's existence. However, this argument is far from the death knell of theism (belief in the existence of a god) in general and certainly does not defeat Christianity. Though this argument fails to accomplish what the atheist and the skeptic hope, it does speak to one of humanity's greatest questions, albeit from the perspective of a mind that is at enmity with God. The question on so many minds is, why is there suffering in the world? You, dear reader, may ask a more pointed question, why do I suffer? I mentioned the two ladies discussing the tragedy of September 11th already, but we don't have to think that far to find examples of suffering. As I write this section, I am reminded of friends and family who suffered the unexpected horrors brought on by Hurricane Helene. How was a storm able to cause such devastation 300 miles inland? How could this have happened?

So many have repeated the phrase, "I have never seen anything like this." The financial toll and the loss of life are absolutely staggering and many of the questions we have will never be answered in life, but we need not wonder where God is. To quote a country preacher I heard once, "God's not in Heaven wringing His hands and drinking Maalox." Though there are many questions I can't answer, I can tell you that our God is working all things for His glory and the good of His people. If I had the power I would remove your suffering, but if I did, it may be that with the suffering I would remove some eternal blessing our loving Heavenly Father has prepared for you. Trust Him, dear saint. I pray that as we explore the sovereignty of God in the remainder of this chapter, you find a peace only His mighty hands can provide.

The Dilemma Answered: God's Sovereignty

Skeptics of Christianity would argue the believer must answer whether God is able but not willing to end suffering or if He is willing but not able. This presents a false dilemma because the Christian need not choose either option. God is sovereign. This is the answer. God is both able and willing. The dilemma ignores the reality that God has a wise and holy purpose in allowing suffering in this life. Tragically, the prosperity preachers miss the same truth the atheists miss. The atheist denies God's sovereignty. The prosperity teacher, and the fluffy evangelical for that matter, readily acknowledge God's sovereignty, but hold such a stripped-down view of it as to leave God a mere shadow of how Scripture defines Him.

The Definition of Sovereignty

Before we continue, it is necessary to define Sovereignty What do we mean when we say God is sovereign? A.W. Pink, one of the most prolific preachers of grace in modern times defined God's sovereignty as well as anyone ever has. Pink declares,

> *"To say that God is Sovereign is to declare that God is God. To say that God is Sovereign is to declare that He is the Most High, doing according to His will in the army of Heaven, and among the inhabitants of the earth, so that none can stay His hand or say unto Him what doest Thou?." Dan. 4:35*

To say that God is Sovereign is to declare that He is the Almighty, the Possessor of all power in Heaven and earth so that none can defeat His counsels, thwart His purpose, or resist His will (Psa. 115:3). To say that God is Sovereign is to declare that He is "The Governor among the nations" (Psa. 22:28), setting up kingdoms, overthrowing empires, and determining the course of dynasties as pleaseth Him best. To say that God is Sovereign is to declare that He is the "Only Potentate, the King of kings, and Lord of lords" (1 Tim 6:15). Such is the God of the Bible" (Pink, 1949). Isaiah 45 describes God's choice to appoint Cyrus, the founder of the Perian Empire, as the means of delivering Israel from Babylon. Isaiah's prophesy declares,

"Thus saith the LORD to his anointed, to Cyrus, whose right hand I have holden, to subdue nations before him; and I will lose the loins of kings, to open before him the two leaved gates; and the gates shall not be shut." Isaiah 45:1

The astounding thing about this prophecy is that it was given approximately 150 years before Cyrus ascended the throne. Even more astounding is that Cyrus was an unbeliever. He did not know God and was not aware of this prophesy when he liberated Israel. Verse four of the chapter explains that God called Him when he still knew not God so that all Israel would know Jehovah is the one true God. It is believed that Cyrus did eventually come to faith under the influence of Daniel (Ezra 1:2). God did all of this in order to display His glorious sovereignty over all. Verses 7-13 provide a glorious description of God's sovereignty. Notice God's declaration concerning Himself. I am the LORD, and there is none else, there is no God beside me: I girded thee, though thou hast not known me: That they may know from the rising of the sun, and from the west, that there is none beside me. I am the LORD, and there is none else. I form the light, and create darkness: I make peace, and create evil: I the LORD do all these things (Isaiah 45:5-7). Both light and darkness are created by God. Well-being and calamity flow through the hands of His almighty providence. All things are under His control. The book of Amos contains an equally strong reference to God's absolute Sovereignty.

"Shall a trumpet be blown in the city, and the people not be afraid? Shall there be evil in a city, and the LORD hath not done it?" Amos 3:6

The Extent of God's Sovereignty

We should not conclude from these powerful declarations that God is the author of evil. God's decree does not violate the will of the creature, does not eliminate second causes, and does not make God responsible for the sins of man though He is sovereign over all. Notice how chapter three, paragraph one of The Baptist Confession of 1689 describes the decree of God.

"From all eternity God decreed everything that occurs, without reference to anything outside himself. He did this by the perfectly wise and holy counsel of his own will, freely and unchangeably. Yet God did this in such a way that he is neither the author of sin nor has fellowship with any in their sin. This decree does not violate the will of the creature or take away the free working or contingency of second causes. On the contrary, these are established by God's decree. In this decree, God's wisdom is displayed in directing all things, and his power and faithfulness are demonstrated in accomplishing his decree." Press, 2017

The confession lists numerous proof texts for this doctrine, but I will only mention two of them here, Isaiah 46:10, and Ephesians 1:11.

"Declaring the end from the beginning, and from ancient times the

things that are not yet done, saying, My counsel shall stand, and I will do all my pleasure" Isaiah 46:10

In whom also we have obtained an inheritance, being predestinated according to the purpose of him who worketh all things after the counsel of his own will" (Ephesians 1:11).

Nothing happens outside the sovereign control of our God. This is a source of great joy for the believer to know that wherever we go we may have confidence that the hands of providence guide us all the way. Scripture declares God to be sovereign over the salvation of the elect (Ephesians 1:4,9; Romans 8:30; Romans,9:13). He is sovereign over creation (Hebrews 1:3; Colossians 1:17). He is sovereign over the affairs of men and nations (Psalm 22:28; Proverbs 21:1, Daniel 4:17). God is even sovereign over the sins of man. Truly if God did not grant man the power to sin, he would not be able to. God withheld Abimelech from being with Sarah (Genesis 20:6). He also prevented Joseph's brothers from killing him (Genesis 37: 21-24). God did not keep Adam from sinning but could have if He had willed to. God could have softened the heart of Pharoah so that he would allow Israel to go, but He withheld the grace necessary for Pharoah to hear the word of God. So then when man sins, it is because God has willed not to prevent it.

If God is sovereign over all things, we can rest assured He is sovereign over our suffering as well. Satan desired to destroy Job but had to go through God before he could do anything. God permitted this attack and Job rightly concluded his suffering to come from the hand of God. It is evident that God had a far different purpose in Job's suffering than Satan. Saint, God's purposes for you are good and holy. I have heard many say that God wants to heal everyone. Rest assured dear believer, If God wanted to heal you, you would be healed. No power can stop the will of God. Paul prayed for God to remove his thorn in the flesh, but God promised that His grace would be sufficient. We will study Paul's thorn in the flesh in a later chapter, but Scripture does not obscure the fact that Paul's infirmity was in his flesh and was from God.

> *"And he said unto me, My grace is sufficient for thee: for my strength is made perfect in weakness. Most gladly therefore will I rather glory in my infirmities, that the power of Christ may rest upon me. Therefore I take pleasure in infirmities, in reproaches, in necessities, in persecutions, in distresses for Christ's sake: for when I am weak, then am I strong."*
> 2 Corinthians 12:9-10

Objections to Sovereignty

Few doctrines strike at the pride of man more than the sovereignty of God. This doctrine has been the subject of great controversy throughout church history, but it is difficult to see how someone who gives Scripture an honest reading could ignore this glorious truth which is a beacon of strength, joy, and comfort for the believer.

Most often those who object to God's sovereignty will cite the free will of man. The argument is that if God's sovereignty is as we describe it, then man cannot have free will. The golden calf of free will has become the stumbling block for many. It was once stated to me that if God is sovereign man can't have free will and if man has free will then God cannot be sovereign. If this were true, prophecy would not be possible. The prophet Micah could foretell the place of Christ's birth, but God would have no power to accomplish it since man must remain free. Sovereignty assures that all God speaks will surely come to pass. Men are not forced to act in one way or the other, but not one of God's decrees will fail. This cannot be, some would object. But it cannot be any other way. How could Christ be a lamb slain from the foundation of the world if God is not sovereign? He would not be able to ensure the actions of men. How could God have withheld the hand of Abimelech if He is not Lord over all? If He were not absolutely sovereign, He would have no power to accomplish His will, man would veto power over God.

Does teaching the sovereignty of God lead to fatalism? If God is sovereign why pray? If God is sovereign why witness? If God is sovereign why work? God has indeed ordained the ends. That cannot be denied, but He has also ordained the means. The same God who assures us He knew His people from eternity past commands us to go and tell all people and also commands all men everywhere to repent. The same God who has charted the course of the universe and will accomplish all His will also promises that the effectual, fervent prayer of a righteous man avails much. God is sovereign and man is responsible. This is a tension we must hold even if it is one we cannot grasp.

It is further objected that the sovereignty of God makes God the author of sin. This too requires us to maintain the tension between God's sovereignty and man's responsibility. Stephen Charnock is especially helpful on this point.

To say God doth will sin as he doth other things is to deny his holiness; to say it entered without anything of his will is to deny his omnipotence. If he did necessitate Adam to fall, what shall we think of his purity? If Adam did fall without any concern of God's will in it, what shall we say of his sovereignty? The one taints his holiness, and the other clips his power. If it came without anything of his will in it, and he did not foresee it, where is his omniscience? If it entered whether he would or not, where is his omnipotence? "Who hath resisted his will?" (Rom. 9:19). "There cannot be a lustful act in Abimelech if God will withhold his power: "I withheld thee" (Gen. 20:6) nor a cursing word in Balaam's mouth, unless God give power to speak it: "Have I now any power at all to say anything? The word that God puts in my mouth, that shall I speak" (Num. 22:38). As no action could be sinful if God had not forbidden it, so no sin could be committed if God did not will to give way to it" (Charnock, 2024).

Our Response to Sovereignty

May this wonderful truth lead us to a deeper sense of awe over the majesty of our God. May it deepen our love for the one who set His love on us from eternity, and cause us to worship Him in a greater way. Above all, this truth should lead to a greater humility and wonder that the sovereign

King of the universe would think on us. He has made us His own, assures us He is working all things for our good, and promises to complete the work began in us.

> *"Such knowledge is too wonderful for me; it is high, I cannot attain unto it." Psalm 139:6*

3
Suffering Through the Crucible

"For unto you, it is given on behalf of Christ, not only to believe in him, but also to suffer for his sake." Philippians 1:29

"Poor Cinderelly. Every time she finds a minute, that's the time when they begin it! Cinderelly! Cinderelly!" (Wilfred Jackson, 1950). The lamentation of Jaq, the mouse, from Disney's cinematic treasure Cinderella, perfectly captures the human response to suffering. Cinderella is compelling because we are drawn in by the quiet suffering of the heroine at the hands of her vindictive stepmother, and spiteful step sisters. If Cinderella had been loud, aggressive, and ill-tempered we would not have minded her mistreatment. We may have even concluded she was getting what she deserved. Our response to suffering is based on our perception of injustice. Someone innocent is suffering wrongly.

Every time the hero gunslinger in the greatest movie genre (the American Western) gets the drop on a despicable villain we enjoy the justice being handed out. We don't mind suffering when someone is getting their just deserts. When someone suffers due to their folly, we may feel bad for them, but we don't object to the reality of suffering. Our problem comes when someone who is seemingly innocent suffers due to no fault of their own. When a young mother is stricken with cancer or a child is killed by a drunk driver we cry out for answers. Underserved suffering is revolting. We mourn over what seems to be a grave injustice. In this response, we reveal a flaw in our understanding. We are finite, fallen, and shortsighted.

Our sin-tainted intellect does not allow us to see things as they are. Oh that we would have the mind of Job saying "Shall we receive good at the hand of God and not evil?" (Job 2:10) We fail to acknowledge we all deserve eternal wrath, so whatever may be said of our suffering it cannot be said that God has not been gracious to us. David Jones and Russell Woodbridge provide a helpful reminder of this truth in their book, Health, Wealth, and Prosperity: How the Prosperity Gospel Overshadows the Gospel of Christ. The authors point out that,

> *"While a given instance of suffering may not be deserved (in the sense that it was not caused by one's own immediate sin) when compared to the eternal condemnation that all people ultimately deserve for their sin, charges of divine inequity quickly dissipate. Given the grace that the Lord affords sinful humanity in His mercy, such consideration ought to move one to praise God who 'hows his love for us in that while we were still sinners, Christ died for us.' Romans 5: 8"*
> *Woodbridge, 2017*

That answer may not seem helpful to many, but we must

come to an understanding of the theology that underlies our suffering. Faithful Christians readily acknowledge the truth of human sinfulness and its role in suffering. We acknowledge our own sinfulness. Nevertheless, the theological implications of the fall don't answer our question. In other words, the answer of a seminary professor, though correct, may not always help. We long for the words of our loving Savior who bids all come to Him for rest. We want to know; we need to know if there is any purpose to all the suffering we see and especially the suffering we experience. This is partly why we accept the suffering of villains and reject the suffering of the seemingly innocent. We can accept when there is a point, purpose, or bond in suffering. We cannot accept abstract suffering that is devoid of meaning. Was there meaning in Cinderella's suffering? Is there meaning in our suffering? Does God have a purpose in allowing suffering or are we to simply hang tough until the end?

For His Glory

God allows suffering for His glory. On the surface that thought may not sound all that comforting. Imagine sitting next to a distraught mother who has just lost her young child for reasons she can't explain and is doubtful she would truly understand or accept it in this life. If we were to sit down next to that crying, confused, and weary mother and say to her, "Rejoice! God intends this for His glory," the reaction would be anything other than joy and regardless of our intentions, our words in that moment would prove to be heartless and hurtful. The technical truth doesn't provide comfort in the depths of our wounds. So far, we have focused on technical answers to the problem of evil. While all answers to this dilemma are theological in nature, some seem to be more practical than others. Though that be true, this same mother, given time, the ministry of the Word, and the comfort of the Holy Spirit will come to apprehend the sublime yet perplexing truth that even the most tragic calamity is for God's glory.

Scripture declares the truth that all things exist for the glory of our great God and Savior Jesus Christ.

"The LORD hath made all things for himself: yea, even the wicked for the day of evil." Proverbs 16:4

John the Beloved in describing the Heavenly scene records,

"Thou art worthy, O Lord, to receive glory and honor and power: for thou hast created all things, and for thy pleasure they are and were created." Revelation 4:11

Paul the Apostle rejoiced in the truth that,

"For of him, and through him, and to him, are all things: to whom be glory forever. Amen" Romans 11:36

As believers we echo Martha who when hearing Jesus proclaim Himself to be the resurrection acknowledged her trust that Lazurus would rise on the last day (John 11:24). Jesus was telling Martha that the resurrection is a present reality. In much the same way, God's glory is now. God manifests His glory through His works, in the Church, and through His people.

When we suffer Biblically, we display God's glory to the world. Chelsea Patterson Sobolik explains,

"When we respond to suffering well, we practically demonstrate to the unbelieving world that Christ is more glorious and precious to us than any pain and difficulty we might endure. We have the opportunity to show where and in whom we find our true treasure. By placing our ultimate hope in Christ rather than in the temporary things of this world, God receives the glory." Sobolik, 2014

When we receive the suffering of this life with patience, joy, and a heart of submission to our glorious savior, we proclaim God's glory. We proclaim there is nothing better than Jesus. We sing of His glory. We preach His glory. We show that His grace is sufficient, but when we wade through the deep waters of suffering all the while still singing that God is faithful, it is then that the world sees those truths on full display.

When my Dad witnessed my precious mother leave this world to behold the face of God, he exulted in a tearful voice, "O Father, we know you do all things well!" I suppose I have recounted that story while preaching as much or perhaps more than any other experience in my life. More than all the vacations we took, the gifts I received from my parents, and more than anything else, that memory is forever in my mind as clearly as though it happened yesterday. Truth be told, I only remember one or two of our vacations, and most of the gifts I receive are forgotten with time. But if I live to be one hundred years old, that memory rings forever clearly in my mind. On that day God used my Dad to show me His glory as I had never witnessed it.

On this point, the prosperity preachers swing and miss. It is folly to proclaim the value of health and wealth. Many who experience health and wealth have never given one-second thought to God's glory. No one has ever looked at Kenneth Copeland's home, suits, jets, and savings and proclaimed, "God is good!" Many however have witnessed a suffering saint raise their hands in praise to God even while mourning the loss of loved ones and have been transported to transcendent thoughts of God's surpassing glory. Take heart, dear saint, God is revealing His glory through you

> *"For our light affliction, which is but for a moment, worketh for us a far more exceeding and eternal weight of glory; While we look not at the things which are seen, but at the things which are not seen: for the things which are seen are temporal; but the things which are not seen are eternal."*
>
> *2 Corinthians 4:17-18*

Conform Us to Christ

When she was a small child, my sister sang the song, "He's Still Working on Me." It is doubtful she understood the significance of what she was singing at such a young age, and given her humility, it is equally doubtful she realizes how great His work has been in her life. The simple children's song reminds us of the powerful truth that God is in the process of working with us. We are His workmanship. The moment you trusted Christ, God began conforming you into the image of His dear Son. Notice this truth so wonderfully spelled out in the epistle of Romans. Paul writes,

"For whom he did foreknow, he also did predestinate to be conformed to the image of his Son, that he might be the firstborn among many brethren." Romans 8:29

You and I are being made Christ-like. You may not recognize it and you may lament over what you perceive to be a lack of growth, but you are growing. I see it in the lives of the many the Lord has enabled me to minister to. Don't fret if you don't recognize it. I don't think I ever noticed my growth as a child, but I know my mother did. She would often exclaim the reality that it was difficult to keep me in clothes that fit. Make no mistake, God is transforming you into the likeness of Christ.

But how is this done? We know the Word shapes us and conforms us, but this is not the only means. God has ordained suffering for this eternal purpose. I would often complain of my shins hurting when I was young. I was experiencing growing pains and in my immature mind, the pain was disturbing. My mother never explained the science to me. She simply gave me a glass of milk, spoke some words of comfort to me, and sent me back to bed. Though I am not a scientist, I am pretty sure there is no correlation between milk and the relief of growing pains. In all likelihood, it was maternal love that eased my pain. Pain is a natural part of growing and this is true both physically and spiritually.

We will not escape suffering in this life. Even the Lord Jesus learned and grew through suffering. Jesus though fully God, is also fully human. Consequently, he learned, grew, and suffered like all men. The author of Hebrews points out this truth when he states,

> *"Though he were a Son, yet learned he obedience by the things which he suffered." Hebrews 5:8*

In one respect Christ as God always knew obedience. As a man, however, he learned practically what it meant to obey. As a man, Christ experienced obedience through the things He suffered. This was necessary for Him to become our great High priest. When we suffer, we learn obedience just as Christ did.

How are we to learn to be humble as Christ is? How do we learn to patiently endure as He did? How do we learn to trust the Father as He did? We will not learn these things apart from suffering. Peter declared,

> *"For even here unto were ye called: because Christ also suffered for us, leaving us an example, that ye should follow his steps: Who did no sin, neither was guile found in his mouth: Who, when he was reviled, reviled not again; when he suffered, he threatened not; but committed himself to him that judgeth righteously."* 1 Peter 2:21-23

Rather than reacting adversely, seeking revenge, and demanding fair treatment Christ suffered quietly committing Himself to the Father's care. In doing so, Christ not only purchased our redemption but left us an example since Christ is our example in these things, it is inconceivable that we should go through life without suffering. We take joy in suffering because we know God is working in us something of eternal value.

Strengthen Our Faith

My High School weight lifting teacher, Coach Morgan, would often remind us that you can't build muscle without pain. He taught me and a friend the harsh reality of this truth after we decided to skip class on a day we deemed to be too unpleasant to attend. The class was in trouble for something, so rather than bear the punishment, Freddie, or Fred Head as I affectionately called him, I skipped class. When we returned to class the following day, Coach Morgan looked at me and shouted. "Kuykendall!" On that day I learned not to try and outsmart Coach Morgan, but once the pain subsided I also learned the value of a difficult workout. The reality is there are some things we will never learn without suffering. Elizabeth Elliot in recounting the trying experience of losing her husband, a missionary who was murdered by the Auca Indians asserts,

> *"I learned in that experience who God is. Who He is in a way that I could never have known otherwise. And so, I can say to you that suffering is an irreplaceable medium through which I learned an indispensable truth. I Am. I am the Lord. In other words, that God is God." Elliot, 2019*

The trials of suffering reveal to us the value of our faith.

> *"That the trial of your faith, being much more precious than of gold that perisheth, though it be tried with fire, might be found unto praise and honour and glory at the appearing of Jesus Christ." 1 Peter 1:7*

Peter explains to his readers that the trial of our faith is more precious than gold. That is, it is good that we suffer. When gold is placed into the furnace, the impurities are removed and the genuineness of the gold is revealed. The fire proves the gold to be true. The heat of the crucible remove any impurity from the gold. Similarly, the trials of life reveal to us how precious our faith is. We hear Sunday after Sunday that God's grace is sufficient. We are told that God will carry us through difficult times and even in the darkest trials, the glory of His presence shines through. It is proclaimed from pulpits that God's people persevere, or to state it another way, He who began a good work in you will bring it to completion in the day of Christ Jesus (Philippians 1:6).

We hear those things and by faith give assent to the truthfulness of God's Word, but it isn't until we are placed through the crucible that we learn these truths experientially. If you have experienced trials and your faith is still intact, this should be enough for you to rejoice because the opposite is true for the reprobate. For these people, trials do not strengthen their faith. They do not see the glory of God nor do they learn God's faithfulness, instead they reject the faith, wallow in bitterness, express their hatred of God, and embrace a morally corrupt lifestyle. Their end is worse than their beginning (Matthew 12:43-45). These are the ones our Savior spoke of who embraced the gospel at first, but because the soil is not good, the Word is taken away from them, and whatever fruit they appeared to possess dried up (Mark 10:1-20).

But this is not so of you. The grace of God is at work in your life and the fruit remains. Rejoice! God has allowed suffering in your life to show you things you could not have known otherwise and you are eternally better for it. Suffering is unpleasant here, but if we could see the glorious, eternal results, we would gladly march through whatever God sends our way.

> *"But, beloved, we are persuaded better things of you, and things that accompany salvation, though we thus speak. For God is not unrighteous to forget your work and labour of love, which ye have*

shewed toward his name, in that ye have ministered to the saints, and do minister." Hebrews 6:9-10

Look to Him

God uses suffering to draw our focus, faith, and attention back to him. C.S. Lewis in his uniquely masterful way said,

"God whispers to us in our pleasures, speaks in our conscience, but shouts in our pain: it is His megaphone to rouse a deaf world." Elliot, 2019

In our suffering, God directs our gaze toward Him. Skeptics charge this makes God a megalomaniac, but such an accusation is not only blasphemous it's incredibly shortsighted. In looking to God and fixing our attention on Him we receive our highest good, our greatest joy, and most glorious reward. Coach Morgan was not a bad coach for training us to endure the suffering of the weight room. He was just the opposite. He was a good coach desiring his students to grow meeting our full potential. Coach Morgan had a long-term perspective. How much greater God's desire and perspective! It is for our benefit that He through trials causes our gaze to be directed to Him. The author of Hebrews reminds us of this blessed truth when he writes,

"Furthermore we have had fathers of our flesh which corrected us, and we gave them reverence: shall we not much rather be in subjection unto

the Father of spirits, and live? For they verily for a few days chastened us after their own pleasure; but he for our profit, that we might be partakers of his holiness. Now no chastening for the present seemeth to be joyous, but grievous: nevertheless afterward it yieldeth the peaceable fruit of righteousness unto them which are exercised thereby."
Hebrews 12:9-11

Suffering is sometimes how God draws the sinner to Himself. It was through the pains of suffering that the prodigal son was moved to return to the Father. The clear intent of our Lord was to show His mission of saving that which was lost. Through suffering, the prodigal was brought to his right mind. In the hog pen, a penniless, and starving young man came to realize the folly of his way. He concluded his Father's servants had bread enough to spare. This led him to return. He expected to return as a servant because he did not foresee the Father's loving embrace. He expected he would have to earn his way back into the house. Physical pain can lead to eternal joy.

Similarly, God uses suffering to cause His children to redirect their gaze, to fix their eyes on eternal things. In this, He accomplishes the work of sanctification in us and helps us long for eternity with Him. John the Beloved explained,

"And every man that hath this hope in him purifieth himself, even as he is pure." 1 John 3:3

We are so prone to fixate on the temporal. We lose focus and begin to wander away from the Savior. Though we are Christ's we drift into sin and impair the graces of the Christian life. When we drift away our Savior lovingly draws us back into arms. It is His grace that sends us trials so that we may again look to Him and begin once again to strive for the goal.

Rather than grumble when trials come, may we learn to rejoice in the God who does all things well. Pastor Dave Evans, has said that when trials come we ought not ask why, but what." That is, we should seek to know what it is that God wants to learn. We should seek to know where He is directing us. In short, we should trust God and know that He is accomplishing His eternal purpose in us and it will all be worth it when we see His face.

> *"But the God of all grace, who hath called us unto his eternal glory by Christ Jesus, after that ye have suffered a while, make you perfect, stablish, strengthen, settle you. To him be glory and dominion forever and ever. Amen."* 1 Peter 5:10-11

4

Suffering Through Phyiscal Ailments

"And lest I should be exalted above measure through the abundance of the revelations, there was given to me a thorn in the flesh, the messenger of Satan to buffet me, lest I should be exalted above measure. For this thing, I besought the Lord thrice, that it might depart from me. And he said unto me, My grace is sufficient for thee: for my strength is made perfect in weakness. Most gladly therefore will I rather glory in my infirmities, that the power of Christ may rest upon me. Therefore I take pleasure in infirmities, in reproaches, in necessities, in persecutions, in distresses for Christ's sake: for when I am weak, then am I strong." 2 Corinthians 12:7-10

On cold fall days, my wife and I would dress warmly to watch our youngest daughter, Lindsey compete in cross country. Through winding trails, hills, mud, and physical exhaustion, she pushed through as she focused on the goal. The finish line, which seemed such a great distance away, is what encouraged her to push through the pain and overcome obstacles. The encouragement she received from her parents, friends, teammates, and coaches was certainly a great help, but none of us could have prompted her to ignore the pain and to keep putting one foot in front of the other had there been no purpose or end goal. So often as I watched her graceful display of endurance, and listened to all the shouts of encouragement, I couldn't help but see a parallel to the Christian life. The cross-country race is not dissimilar to our journey, is it? We endure endless struggles as we push toward the goal knowing the glory we will enjoy far outweighs the struggle (Romans 8:18). The life of the Apostle Paul is a great example of this joyful endurance.

Paul's thorn in the flesh has been the subject of much debate. The argument centers around what exactly Paul intends to communicate by the phrase, "thorn in the flesh." The imagery employed by the Apostle is used in two other places in Scripture, Joshua 23:13, and Ezekiel 28:24. In these passages the phrase describes the enemies of Israel rather than the physical ailment that I will argue Paul is describing. Judges 2:3 may also be listed as an Old Testament reference, but the word "thorns" is supplied by our translators in that text and some translations have opted for a different reading. At any rate, the phrase would have been at least vaguely familiar to Paul's readers. It seems that Paul's use of the image is the one most commonly recalled by today's readers. The image of a thorn in the flesh is certainly compelling. So compelling in fact that this word picture has found its way into classic and modern literature and even our modern parlance. We use words to describe an annoying or difficult person, a physical ailment, an unfinished task, or any difficulty we may face. We understand the principle of what Paul is saying then, but the argument is over what exactly this thorn represents.

Was God unkind for allowing Paul to suffer? Was it

unbecoming of God to allow this? Not when we consider the eternal benefits suffering accomplished for Paul. We accuse God of being cruel because we are shortsighted. All He does is for the good of His people and His glory. This is not to say that suffering in and of itself is good, but that through our suffering God accomplishes good. So, this suffering came by the hand of God. It is true that Paul refers to this thorn as the messenger of Satan. Suffering in Scripture is often attributed to the agency of Satan and Paul indicates, in this case, God allowed Satan to afflict him. We should not however take the phrase "the messenger of Satan" as an identification of the thorn itself, but rather a description of the thorn. As it were, the thorn was a messenger of Satan, but this should not lead us to conclude that the thorn itself referred to a demonic messenger. God allowed Satan to afflict Paul. This was also the case with Job. Satan afflicted Job, but he had to go through God to get to Job. Satan's purpose for Job was far different than God's. Such was the case for Paul. God intended it for Paul's spiritual benefit even though Satan's intentions were no doubt malicious. Christian, if you are suffering be assured God intends this for your good.

The question still remains as to what this thorn is. What does Paul have in view when he refers to his suffering as a thorn in the flesh? John Calvin held the view that this thorn referred to the many temptations Paul faced. Though I hold Calvin in high regard, his view on this is disappointing. Temptations are common to all believers. We are all prone to face temptation and it seems inconceivable that Paul would list temptations as something unique to him. Furthermore, I do not believe it can be argued that God would send temptations into Paul's life. James reminds us that God is neither tempted nor does he tempt any man. Temptations are rather a product of our sinful desires (James 1:13-15). Some have suggested that this thorn specifically refers to lust that Paul struggled with. This view is reprehensible, and I struggle to contrive a charitable response to such folly, so I will simply say it is an error of judgment to make such a claim. It seems reasonable to question the motive behind such a profoundly ridiculous claim. Many noted scholars believe this thorn refers to the various enemies of the gospel Paul faced everywhere he went. This view was notably propounded by John Chrysostom (349-407), one of the most important early church fathers. This view should also be rejected since opposition and persecution were not novel to Paul. Indeed, Christians throughout the ages have faced persecution and opposition. Furthermore, if Paul intended his word picture to point to the enemies of the gospel this would have been a strange way to phrase it. Biblical scholar Sam Storms observes,

> "If Paul had his opponents in mind, he chose an especially obscure way to make his point." Storms, 2008

Given the context, this thorn must refer to a physical ailment. The wording is simple. There was given to me a thorn in the flesh. Charles Hodge explains,

"Flesh may be taken literally for the body, or figuratively for the corrupt nature. Calvin and many others take the latter view. But there is no reason for departing from the literal meaning, which should in all cases be preferred, other things being equal."
Hodge, 1857,2023

Hodge's argument is bolstered by Paul's statement in verse 9 after his prayer and the Lord's refusal to remove the thorn.

"And he said unto me, My grace is sufficient for thee: for my strength is made perfect in weakness. Most gladly therefore will I rather glory in my infirmities, that the power of Christ may rest upon me."
2 Corinthians 12:9

Notice Paul exults, that he will glory in his infirmities. It seems to me that Paul tells us his thorn was a bodily ailment and we should believe him. This thorn then cannot be temptation, enemies of the gospel, or even a demon since the natural reading of the text demands the thorn to be an ailment in the Apostle's flesh.

We have settled on the fact that this thorn was a physical ailment, but we still don't know the exact nature of this thorn. Various maladies have been proposed all with some degree of merit, but the most convincing is that Paul's illness was related to his eyesight. In Galatians 4, Paul seems to refer to an issue with his eyes that gave the Galatians the opportunity to show greater love to him. Notice Paul's words.

"Ye know how through infirmity of the flesh I preached the gospel unto you at the first. And my temptation which was in my flesh ye despised not, nor rejected; but received me as an angel of God, even as Christ Jesus. Where is then the blessedness ye spake of? for I bear you record, that, if it had been possible, ye would have plucked out your own eyes, and have given them to me." Galatians 4:13-15

Though he does not specifically state the infirmity affected his eyes, it is noted that the Galatians would have given their own eyes to him if it were possible. It is possible that Paul was using figurative language, but it is not unwarranted to infer that Paul was speaking of his eyesight. This idea is also supported by Paul's difficulty identifying the high priest in Acts 23:3-5. Given Paul's background, he would have been able to identify the high priest easily by his garments unless his eyesight prevented him. We can't say for certain what exactly Paul's thorn was and maybe it's best that way.

This passage clearly shows that God allows His people to suffer for His glory and our good. This is not to say that the entire argument stands or falls on this passage, but there is a great deal to learn from this text. Through his suffering, Paul gained invaluable insight into not only himself but the grace of God. I pray we are able, like Paul, to take hold of these same insights. There are three lessons I want us to focus on in this section: The human heart is inclined towards pride, God graciously uses suffering to humble us, and through suffering, we learn true joy.

The Human Heart is Inclined Towards Pride

We are all dangerously inclined towards pride. From the little league athlete to the fisherman, the successful executive, and the blue-collar worker we are all susceptible to becoming prideful. What then is the source of this pride? The answer is sin. Our fallen, sinful nature inclines us towards pride. The prophet Isaiah described our sinful state succinctly when he wrote,

"All we like sheep have gone astray; We have turned, everyone, to his own way; And the LORD has laid on Him the iniquity of us all."
Isaiah 53:6

When man fell in the garden he was set on a destructive path away from God. We go astray because we believe we can live life apart from God. We choose our path because we arrogantly believe we can chart our course, make our way, and lead ourselves to success. We do not believe we are foolish and self-destructive. We are wise in our conceit. We are just like our father Adam who spurned the loving guidance of his Creator and chose his lust instead. This is the epitome of sinful human nature. Divorce rates are as high as they are because we have chosen our path. We see the marks of our destructive choices all around us. The sexual revolution has torn apart the family unit, increased disease, and all manner of human suffering because we choose our path. We are so bent on pride that we dedicate an entire month to it. Pride month is a testimony to our rebellion. We will not have Christ as our king (Luke 19:14).

But the sexual deviants who celebrate pride month don't have the market cornered on pride. Many heterosexual, cultural Christians will castigate the horrors of the LGBTQ movement while they rebel against the Biblical ethic. In their pride, they have chosen a sin more respectable in their own eyes. Pride is ingrained into the human heart. We do not need a King to reign over us. Just be there when it suits our emotional response and we will be happy.

The Origin of Pride

This tendency to pride is more pernicious than we imagine though. Pride did not originate in the human heart but is Satanic in origin. Notice the words of Isaiah.

> *"For you have said in your heart: 'I will ascend into heaven, I will exalt my throne above the stars of God; I will also sit on the mount of the congregation On the farthest sides of the north; I will ascend above the heights of the clouds, I will be like the Most High."*
> Isaiah 14:13-14

Though we never assume to mount a mutiny against the Creator, we assume His rightful place each time we sin because in doing so we raise our will against His.

Despite our pride and rebellion, God has had mercy on us. In Genesis 3, God promised his fallen creatures a redeemer. This promise was fulfilled in the person of Christ and those of us who have trusted in Christ enjoy the forgiveness of sins and are now part of God's family. Ironically, this divine favor can often increase our tendency to pride. This is especially true for those who have seen an abundance of God's favor. This is why Paul instructed the Corinthians to only glory in the Lord (2 Corinthians 10:17). Paul understood this danger all too well. He had been the recipient of extraordinary divine favor. So great was the extent of revelation he received that he was caught up to Heaven itself. (2 Corinthians 12:2)

In 2 Corinthians 12, Paul describes this experience and though we cannot tell on what occasion this happened, it is clear that he was caught up into Heaven. What Paul saw during this time was so great he could not speak of it. Paul, of course, understood enough to know it would be folly for him to become prideful over those things God had graciously done on his behalf. He even reminded the Corinthians, on another occasion, to be mindful that God was the source of all their blessings. All that we have is from the gracious hand of our God.

"For who maketh thee to differ from another? and what hast thou that thou didst not receive? now if thou didst receive it, why dost thou glory, as if thou hadst not received it?"
1 Corinthians 4:7

God Graciously Uses Suffering to Humble Us

"And lest I should be exalted above measure through the abundance of the revelations, there was given to me a thorn in the flesh, the messenger of Satan to buffet me, lest I should be exalted above measure."
2 Corinthians 12:7

In all likelihood, the Corinthians knew about Paul's ailment and knew exactly what he meant when he discussed his thorn in the flesh. We are years removed from the original writings, so we have to work a little harder when reading the epistle than did the original recipients. The identity of the thorn has been debated, but there are at least two things that should not be debated in these words. We should all agree on the purpose as well as the source of this thorn.

The Apostle pointedly states the purpose of the thorn was to keep him from becoming too prideful. Some translations opt for the term conceited. The idea is that the revelations Paul had received would tend to exalt his pride and cause him to think too highly of himself. Oddly, something God does for us due to His grace would cause us to be prideful, but such is the sinful human condition. How often do we look disdainfully at someone less gifted, intelligent, or capable? How often do we despise the prodigal and falsely assume it is our own wisdom that has kept us out of the hog pen? God saves us, puts us in a wonderful community of believers, and allows us to serve. How could we boast? It is senseless yet we do boast and when we don't boast, we boast in our non-boasting.

God enables us to serve in some capacity and we tend to become prideful in what we have accomplished as though we did it in our strength. Perhaps we do at times perform in our strength. In this case, our pride is an even greater folly. Paul understood this tendency and combatted it. Paul explains to the Galatians,

"But far be it from me to boast except in the cross of our Lord Jesus Christ, by which the world has been crucified to me, and I to the world." Galatians 6:14

This seems to me to be, among other things, evidence that Paul took intentional steps to keep pride from taking hold of him. Nevertheless, he also came to understand that God must allow suffering into our lives to humble us and conform us to the image of His dear Son.

Some insist suffering never comes from God. These so-called prosperity preachers would have you believe suffering, especially physical suffering, is always an attack by Satan. Creflo Dollar writes, "Biblical prosperity is the ability to control every circumstance and situation in your life. No matter what happens, whether financial, social, physical, marital, spiritual, or emotional, this type of prosperity enables you to maintain control in every situation" (Jr, 1999). Such a statement may sound appealing, but it cannot stand up to scrutiny. A closer look into CrefloDollar's life would no doubt show there are situations beyond his control. His claims simply do not comport with reality. He is not the only one who makes such foolish claims.

The Church is plagued with many false teachers making similar claims. Creflo Dollar isn't the only one pushing this false theology. Joel Osteen may be the most famous, but others such as Benny Hinn, Jesse Duplantis, Kenneth Copeland, and Todd White. Not only does the prosperity gospel defy reality, but it defies Scripture. Was Paul in control of this thorn in the flesh? Was he able to declare victory over this thorn? Even a cursory reading of the text reveals he was not in control. This thorn caused suffering over which he had no control. So, we can be assured that God gave this thorn to Paul for the purpose of keeping him humble, and it may well be that God will allow suffering into our lives for the same purpose.

As we read Paul's words we can be confident that through our suffering God will be glorified in us as we learn to treasure His sustaining grace. Sam Storms beautifully explains,

"If he had been any more specific as to its nature, those who themselves never suffered from the same affliction could easily conclude that the passage has no bearing on their lives. But in leaving the door open, so to speak, concerning the nature of the thorn, each of us is able to identify with Paul's struggle and to learn and grow from how he yielded to the sovereignty and sufficiency of divine grace." Storms, 2008

Suffering Teaches True Joy

By God's grace then we can learn the joy that Paul experienced. Just like Paul, we can rejoice in our infirmities. It is not that our infirmities are cause for rejoicing, but that the end result produces joy. The highest aspiration for the child of God is the glory of God. We learn true joy when we yield ourselves to His sovereign will. When we see that Christ has chosen to manifest His power and presence through us it is then that we see Him for who he truly is and we experience the true joy of knowing Christ. As Charles

Hodges observes, Christianity is not merely the religion which Christ taught; but it is, subjectively considered, the religion of which Christ is the source in the object (Hodge, 1857, 2023). May God give us grace to rest in His love and seek His glory so that we may know true joy.

We can only imagine the difficulty of being an apostle, traveling as an itinerant preacher, missionary, and church planter, all the while suffering from a near-debilitating ailment. Paul prayed earnestly that Christ would remove his near-debilitating pain from Him. Paul's use of the word Lord indicates his prayers were directed to Christ.

> *"For this thing, I besought the Lord thrice, that it might depart from me." 2 Corinthians 12:8*

We should not take from this that Paul only offered three prayers for the removal of this thorn. He is communicating the important nature of his prayer.

It seems to me there were three seasons in which Paul prayed earnestly for the Lord to remove this thorn. This was no brief bedtime prayer. This was a time of earnestly pleading with Christ for this thorn to be taken from him. We can imagine the nature of this prayer and at least try to put ourselves in the ailing preacher's place. How often have we tried to convince God that this thing we desired would be most beneficial for the kingdom? I am sure Paul prayed in this way. Just think of how much more effective he could be if he did not need to rely on others to help him. How much more writing could he do if he did not need to dictate every letter he wrote? When he did write his letter, the size of his writing was nearly impractical (Galatians 6:11). Certainly, his preaching could have been more effective if he had been able to see. How was he supposed to travel around evangelizing with this ailment slowing him down and hindering his progress? Surely the Lord understands! Surely the Lord will remove this thing! He does want me to be as effective as possible and removing this thorn will put me in a place where I can serve most effectively. That's the way we think, isn't it? We arrogantly assume to advise Christ on how he ought to go about building His Kingdom. We cannot see the good in God allowing a thing to go on as it is so we invite ourselves into His Divine Council all the while forgetting that He works all things after the council of His own will (Ephesians 1:11).

Paul was wrong in his belief that this thing should be removed and we often are when we think the same way. May God give us ears to hear His Word! And he said unto me, My grace is sufficient for thee: for my strength is made perfect in weakness. Most gladly therefore will I rather glory in my infirmities, that the power of Christ may rest upon me (2 Corinthians 12:9). The answer Paul received was that God's grace is sufficient. Charles Hodge ably observes,

> *"The connection is in favor of the common meaning of the term. 'My love is enough for thee.' These are the words of Christ. He says to those who seek deliverance from pain and sorrow, 'It is enough that I love you.' This secures and implies all other good his favor is life; His lovingkindness is better than life."* Hodge, 1857,2023

God may choose to remove our suffering, but if He doesn't, we have the assurance that His love for us is enough to sustain us amidst suffering. God's strength is made perfect in our weakness. God does not need our strength. He needs nothing but asks that we depend on Him. We think His Kingdom would benefit most when all obstacles and issues are removed. We do not believe we can serve effectively when we are without strength, but we forget who He is. His strength is revealed in our weakness. Our weakness is the very thing that enables God's strength to be most clearly manifested.

Our strengths may serve to hinder the work of God. Our thoughts are not His thoughts, and our ways are not His (Isaiah 55:8-9). Our wisdom is insufficient, and our strength will never accomplish His eternal purpose. We glorify God when we learn that we are insufficient for the task and must therefore depend on His strength. We may selfishly take His glory, but when God moves through our weakness it is then that we see His glory.

"But we have this treasure in earthen vessels, that the excellency of the power may be of God, and not of us."
2 Corinthians 4:7

5
The Response of Faith

"For even hereunto were ye called: because Christ also suffered for us, leaving us an example, that ye should follow his steps: Who did no sin, neither was guile found in his mouth: Who, when he was reviled, reviled not again; when he suffered, he threatened not; but committed himself to him that judgeth righteously." 1 Peter 2:21-23

When I was young we would have tornado drills in school to prepare us for the unlikely event that a tornado would strike the area of Western North Carolina. The purpose of this was so we would know how to respond if such a tragedy did strike. Similar drills took place in schools during the Cold War Era. The point here is that the time to think about how to respond and prepare is now. Once while playing a game of pickup basketball, a young man who was older and more athletic than me faked a layup and passed the ball to me behind his back. I suppose he thought he was Pistol Pete Maravich or something. I was not prepared for such a pass and the ball hit me square on the face. Maybe he was trying to include me, but I would have preferred he go through with the layup. From then on when playing basketball I prepared myself for such a pass. This preparation never made me a good basketball player, but it did preserve the integrity of my face.

How are we to respond and prepare for suffering? That we will suffer is a given. Some of us may suffer more than others, but it is clear we will not escape suffering in this life. We have addressed the theological concept of suffering and have established from Scripture the reality of suffering in this life, but we need to think about the proper response. You may have drawn inferences from what we have discussed thus far, but it will be beneficial for us to plainly state what our reactions ought to be.

Similarly, we must all think on how we should respond when we are met with trouble. If we observe the teachings of Scripture we will be able to respond in a manner that honors Christ. This doesn't mean our initial reaction won't miss the mark. Indeed, when we are hit with trouble unexpectedly or are treated unfairly our initial response is often less than sanctified. By God's grace and a commitment to truth, however, we can honor our Savior and point others to Him in our suffering.

Following Godly Examples

An example is a powerful teaching tool. I learned how to switch-hit watching someone else. I learned how to pray from my parents. They showed me the importance of being faithful to church, serving in the church, giving to the church, loving the body of Christ, and caring for the wayward. My dad taught me the value of hard work. He taught me how to respond to personal attacks and difficulties. He taught me how to pray and love Jesus. My mom showed me that joy in suffering is possible. She also modeled kindness and affection for me. The value of the example set by my parents cannot be enumerated. I am who I am today in large part because of the example of my parents. Most of what I have learned in the ministry is from other men. Granted I have learned a great deal from my failures, but that is for a different book. Whatever good qualities I possess today are due to the grace of God and the example of those who have walked before me. I am sure we all have examples we are thankful for. My story is not unique in that regard. Thankfully, we also have the examples provided for us in Scripture. Christ is our ultimate example, but I would like to examine some others first.

> *"For whatever was written in former days was written for our instruction, that through endurance and the encouragement of the Scriptures we might have hope."* Romans 15:4

The Apostle Paul instructs us to learn from the example of the Old Testament saints. Their lives display the type of patient endurance and hope we are to employ in our lives. There are perhaps no better examples than Joseph. In his sufferings, he retained his integrity and loyalty to Jehovah. He served faithfully and honestly when he was sold to the Egyptians and placed in Potiphar's house. When falsely accused and put in prison, he served faithfully there. When he was finally released and subsequently promoted he was faithful. Neither trial nor promotion moved Joseph.

We can all think of popular characters from Scripture

who remained faithful in trials. Daniel and his three friends come to mind. We cannot overlook Job whom scripture describes as never sinning with his mouth or charging God foolishly. King David was a man of integrity who trusted God during his trials. Scripture is filled with great men and women whose names will be remembered forever. However, Scripture also provides us with examples of those who are not named. These may be the greatest examples. Notice what the author of Hebrews says of these no names.

> *"And others had trial of cruel mockings and scourgings, yea, moreover of bonds and imprisonment: They were stoned, they were sawn asunder, were tempted, were slain with the sword: they wandered about in sheepskins and goatskins; being destitute, afflicted, tormented; (Of whom the world was not worthy:) they wandered in deserts, and in mountains, and in dens and caves of the earth. And these all, having obtained a good report through faith, received not the promise: God having provided some better thing for us, that they without us should not be made perfect."*
> Hebrews 11:36-40

The author of Hebrews doesn't even provide us with the names of these others and I think it is best that way. We often look at some of the great heroes of the faith and are convinced we could never have faith like that. But, do you think you can be a no-name like these? We can all be a no-name! Many instead of these faithful people are not named, and we can assume they never performed great miracles or other fantastic feats, but they continued in the faith through the unspeakable trials they faced. These others never received the fulfillment of the promises given. God had something better for them that they could not see or understand yet, they continued to be faithful. Not because they understood all that was happening, nor because they saw a reward in this life, but rather because they judged the King of the universe to be worthy of their devotion. May God give us the grace to walk the path of these other saints who, though not mentioned by name, provide a glorious example of patient endurance. As previously stated, the author of Hebrews did not provide us with the name for many of the people he mentioned.

The greatest example provided for us however is the life of Christ. Peter explains in his first epistle that we should follow in the steps of Christ. Our parents, as great as they may be, will fail us. Mentors will let us down. The Old Testament saints we hold in such high regard greatly failed at times. But Jesus never fails. Peter reminded us of this fact when he wrote,

> *"Who did no sin, neither was guile found in his mouth"*
> *1 Peter 2:22.*

There is no greater example than Jesus, but He isn't merely an example, He is our Saviour.

In 1896, Charles Sheldon wrote the classic book In His Steps. In this book, Sheldon tells of a fictitious pastor who encourages his people not to do anything without first considering what Jesus would do. This book has been a blessing to many Christians through the years because the concept is. While some may allow the ideas presented in this classic to descend into a mere social gospel, that need not be the case. Thankfully, we don't have to wonder what Jesus would do since Scripture bears a record of His life. We know how He trusted the Father. We know how he treated others. We know how he responded to suffering. We know how He responded to His persecutors. We know these things and we know how we ought to live. Our Savior was not deterred from His mission nor His trust in the Father. By God's grace, let us walk in the steps of Christ.

Resist the Temptation to Sin in Suffering

For many, suffering unfortunately leads to sin. There is danger in suffering that we would grow cold and indifferent allowing sin to creep into our lives. This is especially true when others are responsible for our suffering. Jesus, as we have already noted, shows us how to respond to suffering. But even when no one is directly responsible for our suffering we may be tempted to sin against God. This sin may be subtle and we may not even realize we are sinning, bus such is the deceptive nature of the human heart.

Sinning with our words may be the greatest temptation in our affliction. We must guard our thoughts and words when we are afflicted. Concerning the response of Christ to suffering, Peter writes,

> *"Who, when he was reviled, reviled not again; when he suffered, he threatened not; but committed himself to him that judgeth righteously."*
> 1 Peter 2:23

When others hurt us, we want to strike back. We want to threaten those who do us harm. But this was not true of Jesus. If anyone has ever suffered unjustly it was our Lord, yet He never lashed out at his accusers. He never threatened them. Jesus suffered in silence and never took the opportunity to defend Himself. We can always convince ourselves that we are justified in letting someone have it verbally. We tell ourselves they deserved it and had it coming. We justify our sinful speech because we are defending ourselves. But we are called to peace and must follow the example of Christ by loving those who hurt us.

Sadly, we often speak harshly to the ones we love when we suffer. They did not cause our pain but still bear the brunt of our wrath. Mary Beeke accurately explains,

> *"In the home setting, we are often less kind to our closest kin... Prayer, self-discipline, instruction from the Bible, and the power of the Holy Spirit are required to bulldoze this character trait into extinction."*
> Beeke, 2007

When we are stressed or troubled, we may be short with our spouse. We may be impatient without children, and we often have unrealistic expectations of them. Our Savior does not treat us this way and we must not treat those we love in this manner. Our Lord is slow to anger and abounding in mercy! How much more should mirror this quality to those we love? Let us take Mary Beeke's advice and surrender this behavior to the Lordship of Christ.

It is unimaginable that we would charge God with our suffering, yet Scripture warns us against that very thing. Job did not sin with his lips or charge God foolishly (Job 1:22). Israel however was a different story. The people of Israel questioned God's goodness in leading them out of Egypt even suggesting they were brought out to die (Exodus 14:11). They complained about the food provided to them in the wilderness (Numbers 21:5). They even complained when brought to the threshold of the promised land (Numbers 13:33). It seems at every turn the Hebrews complained against the hand of providence that led, preserved and protected them. despite having received promises from the God who selected them from among the nations, they complained.

How often do we complain against His providential care? We complain when it rains too much. We complain when it's hot, or cold. We complain when we are stuck in traffic or slightly delayed. Recently, we had the privilege of visiting with family in our home state of North Carolina. It is always a joy to see family and it is a bonus that they all reside in one of the most beautiful places on earth. Whatever joy is present in my heart when I am with family does not diminish my desire to hit the road early when it's time to go. I have never felt the urge to linger. When it's time to visit, we visit and when it's time to go, we go. On this particular trip, we lingered a bit longer than I would have liked to have before leaving. So, I restlessly but quietly waited I hoped to leave an hour earlier, but it just didn't happen. About halfway home we found a section of the interstate closed due to a fatal accident. Had we left when I desired, we may have been caught in that accident. Ultimately, I can't know if we would have been involved in this accident, but I can rest in God's providence instead of being stressed when things don't go exactly my way. Slow traffic and delayed plans pale in comparison to the suffering we all experience, but God is no less present when our path leads through adversity. God sustains us throughout our lives and even when our way is filled with sorrow, we must trust the one who upholds all things by the word of His power (Hebrews 1:3, Acts 17:28).

Bitterness is yet another danger we must guard against. Too many people have allowed the difficulties of life to foster a spirit of bitterness in their souls. Worse yet, this spirit of bitterness if left unchecked will result in unbelief. Professing Christians are often hurt by someone they trust and all too often it is a church leader. Those who have escaped cult-like groups sometimes allow bitterness to take root and blame God for their troubles. This is often the beginning stage of what is now called deconstruction. This is not a new phenomenon, but it has garnered more attention as of late. Suffering is real, and the realities of the hurt should never be diminished but rejecting the Lord of Glory because of affliction is the height of folly. The author of Hebrews warns his readers against a root of bitterness that will spread its rot to any who will countenance this foul spirit.

> "Looking diligently lest any man fail of the grace of God; lest any root of bitterness springing up trouble you, and thereby many be defiled."
> Hebrews 12:15

The one who becomes and stays angry will see the spirit of unbelief, discontentment, and strife flourish in his soul. Once this root of bitterness takes root in one heart, it is like the honeysuckle or the kudzu that never rests until it has dominated all the soil it touches. Don't allow your trials to produce the evil root of unbelief!

Entrust Our Lives to God's Care

> "Who, when he was reviled, reviled not again; when he suffered, he threatened not; but committed himself to him that judgeth righteously"
> 1 Peter 2:23

How can we keep from allowing our trials to introduce sin into our lives? Surely we are not able by our own strength to guard our thoughts and words! Surely we can't will ourselves to follow the examples of those before us. No, it is not through the arm of the flesh that we persevere through trials. It is only through the power of the Holy Spirit that we may with confident trust in God weather the storms of life. If we want to live as those who have gone before us we must possess what they possessed. We must unreservedly entrust our lives to His care. There is only one way to see earthly trials through a heavenly gaze by submission to the Lordship of Christ. Ralph Venning observed,

"Natural men are earthly in the use of heavenly things but spiritual men are heavenly in the use of earthly things."
Smith, 2020

It is helpful in times of sorrow to remember that God's love for us, His special people is infinite. We often forget the depths of His love for us and imagine He is absent when trials come. We must remind ourselves that He loves us with an everlasting love (Jeremiah 31:3). Paul expounds on this incomparable love in Romans 8. See the beautiful promise in these words!

"Who shall separate us from the love of Christ? shall tribulation, or distress, or persecution, or famine, or nakedness, or peril, or sword? As it is written, For thy sake we are killed all the day long; we are accounted as sheep for the slaughter. Nay, in all these things we are more than conquerors through him that loved us. For I am persuaded, that neither death, nor life, nor angels, nor principalities, nor powers, nor things present, nor things to come, Nor height, nor depth, nor any other creature, shall be able to separate us from the love of God, which is in Christ Jesus our Lord."
Romans 8:35-39

Our lot may be to go through the fiercest of trials. We may have to endure famine, nakedness, peril, or sword, but let us remember none of these things will remove us from the love of Christ. He has promised He will never leave us or forsake us (Hebrews 13:5-6). He loves us and is accomplishing His glorious will in us. We bristle at these trials, but we must remember the servant is not greater than his master (John 15:20-22). There is coming a day when our God will make all things new and will wipe all tears away. Things won't always be like they've always been. One day all things will be right and we will rejoice in His presence. Until that day, may God give us grace to rest in His love.

This trust and confidence in God lead us to rejoice even in sorrow that His all-wise council is right. One of the deacons at church, Jim Williams will often pray, "Lord, add your wisdom to these requests." When I first heard him pray that I wasn't sure what to think, but I have learned to love and joy in that prayer. We don't know what is best for us. We do not understand His eternal council. We can't always see what He is doing, but we know He loves us. We know His wisdom is infinite, His knowledge is incomprehensible, His love unfathomable, and His plans consistent with His holy character. This enables us to conclude with the songwriter that whatever God ordains is right.

With this knowledge and God's infinite grace, we may like Christ, entrust our lives to Him that judges rightly. Abraham when praying for Sodom concluded that the judge of all the earth would do right (Genesis 18:25). Our God will one day right the wrongs. Therefore, we need not worry, seek revenge or harbor resentment. He is coming in judgment and will execute perfect justice on that day. When he returns, all the sorrows we faced here will be but a memory as we sing the praises of our Savior on that eternal day in the very presence of the one who is infinitely glorious. Our joy will be perfected then and our bodies made whole, but we don't have to wait until that day to enjoy our Savior. We are promised His love and presence now. We can have His joy now.

> *"Though we now see only in part, what we do see produces blessed joy and satisfaction. Whom having not seen, ye love; in whom, though now ye see him not, yet believing, ye rejoice with joy unspeakable and full of glory." 1 Peter 1:8*

6
Does Jesus Care?

*And the Lord, he it is that doth go before thee; he will
be with thee, he will not fail thee, neither forsake thee:
fear not, neither be dismayed.*
Deuteronomy 3:18

Frank Graeff, a Philadelphia Pastor in the late 1800s and early 1900s was widely known as a joy-filled pastor. It is said that he was nicknamed "The Sunshine Pastor." But it wasn't as though this happy Pastor was shielded from sorrow. Just the opposite is true. Pastor Graeff had great struggles and even suffered from depression at points in his life. In 1901 he was inspired to write the great hymn, "Does Jesus Care?" partly because of the comforting words in 1 Peter 5:7, "Casting all your care upon him; for he careth for you." It is a wonderful truth to consider that our Savior always cares for us even in our sorrows. He is not aloof. He is not a cosmic clock winder. He is intimately aware of the struggles of His children and He cares.

One struggle of the political process is deciding who to vote for. We like to think that the person we vote for understands the predicament of the common man and cares enough to govern accordingly. This is because, as humans, we desire to heard. We want to be understood, and we want choices that are in our best interest. We do not want a detached leader making choices on our behalf. This is also true in the workforce. Many employees lament the fact that their boss just doesn't get it. The reality is that many in positions of authority are far removed from the lives of those in their care. In truth, they don't get it. This however is not true of our Savior. Notice how the prophet Isaiah describes the Son of God.

> *"He is despised and rejected of men; a man of sorrows, and acquainted with grief: and we hid as it were our faces from him; he was despised, and we esteemed him not. Surely he hath borne our griefs, and carried our sorrows: yet we did esteem him stricken, smitten of God, and afflicted." Isaiah 53:3-4*

Jesus is not isolated from our sorrows. He's unlike the leader sitting in his ivory tower enjoying champagne and caviar. Nor is He like the false gods created by the imagination of those who reject the God of the universe. These gods almost always reflect the temperament and flaws of their culture. But, the High and lofty one is holy, transcendent, eternal, all-knowing, all-powerful, and infinite in wisdom. He stepped out of nowhere, stepped on nothing, and by His word, worlds leaped into existence. This is the God we serve and this is the God who cares for us.

Jesus Is A Suffering Savior

Notice again the words of Isaiah.

> *"He is despised and rejected of men; a man of sorrows, and acquainted with grief: and we hid as it were our faces from him; he was despised, and we esteemed him not. Surely he hath borne our griefs, and carried our sorrows: yet we did esteem him stricken, smitten of God, and afflicted." Isaiah 53:3-4*

The prophet refers to our Lord as a man of sorrows. He describes Jesus as being acquainted with grief. When trying to comfort or sympathize with a brother or sister, we often assure them we understand. Sometimes, we are corrected in this language because we do not, in the truest sense of the word, understand. We humans can't always understand exactly what another person is going through. Although we have all experienced grief, that grief is different for each person. But we can remind the individual that while we don't understand, Jesus does understand. Truthfully, there are some things I simply don't understand, but this cannot be said of Christ. He was tempted in all points as we are (Hebrews 4:15). Jesus, as Isaiah prophesied, was "a man of sorrows." In Luke 19 Jesus weeps over the unbelief of Israel. In Matthew 26 we find Jesus expressing deep sorrow at the Garden of Gethsemane prior to His death. The Savior was deeply acquainted with sorrow.

Isaiah does not say that Jesus would be merely one who experienced sorrow. Many of us have experienced sorrow, but it would not be accurate to classify us as a man or woman of sorrow. The greatest sorrow I have experienced in this life is the loss of my mother. This, however, was a moment in time. This is not to diminish suffering, but it is intended to show the temporary nature of suffering. In other words, much of the suffering we experience is confined to a period of time. I suffered the loss of my mother, but the overarching experience of my life has been joy and not sorrow. Many of you can say the same thing. You have experienced sickness, loss, poverty, or any other forms of sorrow, but these trials do not define your entire existence.

The phrase, "man of sorrows' is descriptive of one whose life is marked by suffering. The predominant characteristic of His life was suffering. The idea is that His life was filled with suffering. Proverbs 29:1 describes a man who is often reproved, but it could be translated, "a man of reproof." This describes one whose life is characterized by reproof. Jesus then, in His earthly experience not only experienced suffering, but His life was marked by it. He was a man whose very existence was filled with suffering. John Gill, the 18th-century Reformed Baptist pastor, remarked,

> *"He was known by his troubles, notorious for them; these were his constant companions, his familiar acquaintance, with whom he was always conversant; his life was one continued series of sorrow, from the cradle to the cross." Myers, 2020*

Jesus, unlike us, entered His suffering willingly. The Apostle Paul describes Christ's obedience in Philippians 2:6-8.

"Who, being in the form of God, thought it not robbery to be equal with God: But made himself of no reputation, and took upon him the

form of a servant, and was made in the likeness of men: And being found in fashion as a man, he humbled himself, and became obedient unto death, even the death of the cross."

Jesus willingly laid aside His glory and took on human nature. This does not mean He set aside His essential deity. Christ never ceased to be God, and in His divine nature possessed all the attributes and qualities of deity. He is truly God and truly man. This does mean Christ humbled himself willingly so that He might partake of our nature. He willingly experienced all the suffering and infirmities associated with being human and did so without sin.

"Forasmuch then as the children are partakers of flesh and blood, he also himself likewise took part of the same; that through death he might destroy him that had the power of death, that is, the devil."
Hebrews 2:14

When we think about the humiliation and suffering of Christ we sometimes limit our thoughts to the cross. In doing so, we devalue the suffering of Christ and rob ourselves of the joy of knowing that the Savior identifies with us in suffering. The Baptist Catechism addresses the humiliation of Christ in question 30

> *"Question: Wherein did Christ's humiliation consist? Answer: Christ's humiliation consisted in His being born, and that in a low condition, made under the law, undergoing the miseries of this life, the wrath of God, and the cursed death of the cross, in being buried, and continuing under the power of death for a time."* Barger, 2022

The humiliation of Christ involved far more than His rejection, betrayal, torment, trial, and death. Jesus, the Lord of Glory, willingly took on human nature. He was born with the animals, laid in a manger, and brought up in poverty. The sacrifice His parents offered upon His being presented at the temple was an indication of their poverty (Luke 2:24; Leviticus 12:6-8). As Jesus grew and began his public ministry. He did so in poverty, even indicating he had not have a place of his own to sleep (Matthew 8:20). The Savor understands what it means to do without. He understands hunger, sickness, physical pain, rejection, loneliness, and death. There is no aspect of human existence the Savior is not acquainted with. While many may not understand, Jesus does.

Jesus Is A Sympathetic Savior

> *"For we have not an high priest which cannot be touched with the feeling of our infirmities; but was in all points tempted like as we are, yet without sin. Let us therefore come boldly unto the throne of grace, that we may obtain mercy, and find grace to help in time of need."*
> Hebrews 4:15-16

Because Jesus has experienced our human frailty, He can sympathize with us in our suffering. Rarely have I ever heard the hymn "Does Jesus Care?", that my mind did not carry me to John 11 and the village of Bethany where two sisters waited anxiously on the only one who could help their ailing brother Lazarus. What was keeping Jesus? Surely, He received the message. Why is He not coming? What could be delaying Him? Doesn't He love Lazarus as His frequent visits would indicate? Doesn't He care that we are distressed over this? Does He not understand the situation? Surely, He will come soon. But He didn't come. As the minutes turned into hours, and the hours stretched into days, it became apparent Jesus would not come until Lazarus died of his illness. The disappointment and confusion of Mary and Martha is not difficult to imagine. They had sent for Jesus, the only solution, and were met with silence. They would have to go on and figure out how to get by. Finally, Jesus did come, but He was too late. Both sisters when seeing the Savior lamented that if only, He had been present their brother would not have died.

As Jesus is standing in front of the tomb of Lazarus to raise him from the dead, we are given a clear picture of the heart of Christ. A short, but powerful sentence plainly states, "Jesus wept" (John 11:35). Jesus was not simply sorrowful that Lazarus had died for He knew his friend was about to come out of the grave. Though we cannot be dogmatic, it seems that Jesus wept because he was moved by the sorrow of these two sisters.

> *"For he knoweth our frame; he remembereth that we are dust."*
> *Psalm 103:14*

Jesus does care! Perhaps you have prayed and your situation remains the same and it seems as though the Savior is absent and your requests are denied. We may not receive the answer we desire. We may be asked to walk through situations we would never choose and are unsure we can make it through. We would all love to have Christ speak an authoritative word and remove our sorrow, but we aren't promised that. We can however rest in the knowledge that He stands with us at the grave of our Lazarus and weeps with us. He is a loving Savior who cares for us in our sorrow and bottles all our tears (Psalm 56:8).

Jesus is compassionate because of His nature, but He is also compassionate because of His experience as a man. The author of Hebrews explains that it was necessary for Christ to take on flesh.

> *"Wherefore in all things, it behooved him to be made like unto his brethren, that he might be a merciful and faithful high priest in things pertaining to God, to make reconciliation for the sins of the people. For in that he himself hath suffered being tempted, he is able to succour them that are tempted."* Hebrews 2:17-18

In order for Christ to be the mediator between God and men, He had to be both God and man. Only God can take away sin and destroy the works of the Devil, so our redeemer must be God. But our savior must be a man because only a man could represent fallen humanity before God. Jesus is both God and man is therefore our perfect Savior. John Phillips observes,

> "The Lord Jesus has been made like his brethren so that he can be to us all that we need. We need someone to intercede for us compassionately. He is merciful. We need someone to intercede for us continuously. He is faithful. He can take care of our needs in God's presence." Phillips, 1977,1988

Our Lord has experienced the frailty of the human condition, Therefore, the author of Hebrews, concludes, He is able to help us. Truly, there is not a friend like Jesus! We have read Hebrews 4:15 already, but there is one aspect of that passage that we have yet to notice. Take a look at that verse again, but this time let's include the following verse.

> "For we have not an high priest which cannot be touched with the feeling of our infirmities; but was in all points tempted like as we are, yet without sin. Let us therefore come boldly unto the throne of grace, that we may obtain mercy, and find grace to help in time of need."
> Hebrews 4:15-16

The humiliation of Christ is the grounds upon which we are invited to approach the throne of grace. He is God, so He can hear us and meet our needs. He is a man, so He can sympathize with us in our hour of trouble. We are not promised an escape from our sorrow, but we are promised grace to help. Like Paul, we can testify that His grace is sufficient.

We are often like Hagar who fled from Abram and Sarai (Genesis 16) due to her harsh situation not knowing God had not forgotten her. She was headed back to Egypt because she no doubt concluded the pagans would treat her better than what she was experiencing. But there in the wilderness, Hagar had a face-to-face encounter with the pre-incarnate Christ who assures her of His presence and blessings. Before she returns to Abram and Sarai, she offers a glorious testimony of the God who sees us and is with us.

> *"And she called the name of the LORD that spake unto her, Thou God seest me." Genesis 16:13*

Jesus sees us, is interceding for us, has compassion on us, and invites us to approach His gracious throne. Let us never forget that Jesus does care for us!

Jesus is a Present Savior

The promise for the believer is not just that Jesus cares and intercedes for us, but that He is always present with us. Jesus promised His disciples He would be with them even to the very end of the age (Matthew 28:18-20). The author of Hebrews reminds us of the promise that God would never leave us nor forsake us (Hebrews 13:5). For the disciples who walked with Christ for three and a half years, it may have been difficult to conceive how Jesus could be with them if He was going away.

Since we don't have the visible manifestation of Christ's

presence we may have difficulty with the concept of His presence. The promise of the Savior was that He would be present with His followers through the Holy Spirit. Through the Holy Spirit, Christ is present with us. This concept known as Perichoresis, conveys the truth that where one member of the Trinity is present, the entire Godhead is present because of the essential unity of the Three persons of the Godhead. Before His crucifixion, Jesus assured His troubled disciples as He said,

> *"And I will pray the Father, and he shall give you another Comforter, that he may abide with you forever." John 14:16*

The KJV translates the Greek word *parakleton* as comforter while other translations opts for words such as helper or advocate. In 1 John 2:1, the same word is translated as "advocate." The word refers to one who is called alongside another as an aid. The Holy Spirit walks with us and assists us. He acts in the stead of Christ. R.C. Sproul offers a helpful explanation.

> *"Jesus was saying: "I am not going to leave you helpless. I'm praying to the Father that he will send you one who comes with strength to help you when you are called before magistrates and when death is threatening you. He will help you stand by the power of God."*
> *Sproul, 2009*

Through the Holy Spirit, we have the Savior with us to guide us, help us, and strengthen us for whatever we face. The same Holy Spirit who enabled Peter and Stephen to preach boldly in the face of fierce opposition is the same Holy Spirit who walks with us in every trial.

Not only is Christ present with us through the Holy Spirit, but more than that, He dwells in us. The indwelling presence of Christ is a reality for the believer. Paul writes to the Ephesians,

> *"That Christ may dwell in your hearts by faith; that ye, being rooted and grounded in love" Ephesians 3:17.*

Paul also stated in 2:22 that we are a dwelling place for God. Paul reminded the Corinthians that they were the temple of the Holy Spirit (1 Corinthians 6:19). Those who have been born again by the Spirit of God have the assurance that their Savior abides with them and in them. Christ dwelling in us is not only a present reality for the believer, but it is also a reality we are growing in. Ephesians 3:17 contains not only a declaration but a prayer. Paul's prayer was that Christ may dwell more fully in the hearts of His people. As we learn to rest in Him and His all-sufficient grace, we will find that His presence in us deepens and He becomes the center of all we are. God wants us to grow in grace and in the knowledge of His dear Son. Suffering may be one avenue toward that goal.

> *"I have been crucified with Christ. It is no longer I who live, but Christ who lives in me. And the life I now live in the flesh I live by faith in the Son of God, who loved me and gave himself for me." Galatians 2:20*

It is difficult for us to fully grasp our union with the Savior. The teaching of Scripture is that not only is Christ in us, but we are in Him. We died with Him, were buried with him, have been raised from the dead with Him, and are right now seated in Heavenly places with Him (Romans 6:1-6, Ephesians 2:5-6, Colossians 2:11-12). So close is our union with Christ that Paul connects knowing Him and experiencing the power of His resurrection with suffering. He explains,

> *"That I may know him, and the power of his resurrection, and the fellowship of his sufferings, being made conformable unto his death."*
> *Philippians 3:10*

In our suffering, we grow in the intimate knowledge of our Savior and experience the power that raised Him from the dead. Many of us would readily remove the suffering from our lives, but if we could only see what Christ is accomplishing in us, we would gladly walk through whatever He sends our way. Since you are so vitally and truly connected to Christ, then it must be that He is accomplishing His eternal purposes in you. How could He not intend all things for your good since you are part of His body?

> *"For which cause we faint not; but though our outward man perish, yet the inward man is renewed day by day. For our light affliction, which is but for a moment, worketh for us a far more exceeding and eternal weight of glory; While we look not at the things which are seen,*

but at the things which are not seen: for the things which are seen are temporal; but the things which are not seen are eternal."
2 Corinthians 4:16-18

There is one aspect of Christ's presence that is sometimes, unfortunately, overlooked and that is His presence in the gathered assembly, the Church. Some may insist they need not gather with God's people to worship, but they are only partially right. Though we may and ought to worship privately and with our families, there is a special experience of His presence that we can only know in our fellowship with His body, the Church. Jesus promised,

"For where two or three are gathered together in my name, there am I in the midst of them." Matthew 18:20

Some insist this verse only applies to the Church when it exercises the discipline spelled out in the text, but such rigidity is not warranted by the text. When the Church gathers for the purpose which Christ intended, He is present with us. Paul encouraged the Corinthians that the power of Christ was with them when they met (1 Corinthians 5:4). The Church collectively is the temple of Christ (Ephesians 2:21). When we fellowship around the Word, prayer, singing, and the ordinances, He is present with us. If we neglect any of the gifts Christ has given to His Church we do so to our own detriment. Our Lord knew we would need the Church. The author of Hebrews reminds us of this truth.

"And let us consider one another to provoke unto love and to good works: Not forsaking the assembling of ourselves together, as the manner of some is; but exhorting one another: and so much the more, as ye see the day approaching." Hebrews 10:24-25

We always need the Church, but we especially need the body of Christ when we go through trials.

"Now the God of peace, that brought again from the dead our Lord Jesus, that great shepherd of the sheep, through the blood of the everlasting covenant, Make you perfect in every good work to do his will, working in you that which is well pleasing in his sight, through Jesus Christ; to whom be glory for ever and ever. Amen." Hebrews 13:20-21

7
The Prayer of Faith

"Is any among you afflicted? let him pray. Is any merry? let him sing psalms. Is any sick among you? let him call for the elders of the church; and let them pray over him, anointing him with oil in the name of the Lord: And the prayer of faith shall save the sick, and the Lord shall raise him up; and if he have committed sins, they shall be forgiven him. Confess your faults one to another, and pray one for another, that ye may be healed. The effectual fervent prayer of a righteous man availeth much." James 5:13-16

Is healing for today? As I write this, I am thinking of a young man who attends a church pastored by a dear friend. This young man was a staunch atheist who was diagnosed with a terrible disease. One night, in desperation, he cried out to God, whose existence he had denied his entire life, and asked for healing. He received his healing rapidly and subsequently surrendered to the authority of Christ. God's healing power is a present reality!

Certainly, not everyone receives healing. Nevertheless, God graciously chooses to heal some for His glory. If you are one of God's dear children that He has chosen not to heal, please know He loves you and intends this for your good and His glory. If we are healed, we ought to glorify

God in it. If we are not healed, it should be our desire to be just as resolved to glorify God in our suffering as we would be in our healing.

Those of us who are cessationists (cessationism is the belief that the apostolic gifts have ceased) in our understanding of theology are often accused of doubting the miracle-working power of God, but this simply isn't so. We don't doubt God works miracles today, but we deny that he has vested this power in individuals. We further reject the notion that it is God's will for everyone to be healed in this life. While the young man's healing (mentioned above) was undoubtedly a demonstration of God's power and mercy, it is important to note that this miraculous event occurred not because anyone in the church possessed the gift of healing, but because God, in His sovereignty, chose to heal him for His glory. May God give us grace to honor him in whatever state He places us in so that our response in all things brings glory to Him.

James chapter five is a passage commonly discussed when the subject of healing comes up, but James is more concerned about our prayer life than our healing. The epistle begins with a call to prayer, and in the closing verses, he revisits the subject. In chapter one the elder statesman instructs us to ask God for wisdom if we are lacking (James 1:5), and in chapter four we are told to pray with the right spirit (James 3:3). He comes back to the subject of prayer in chapter five, and focuses on prayers for healing, but he is not only talking about healing. He wants to impress upon us the importance of prayer in all circumstances. Prayer ought to be our first response in all circumstances.

What is your first response when you receive a promotion, have a great day, feel sad or depressed, receive a troubling diagnosis, or have failed greatly? Our first response says a lot about our spiritual maturity. If we desire to be mature Christians we must develop a habit of prayer. Prayer then must be our first response. It may not be our only response, but it ought to be our first. I pray as we examine this text, we are stirred to make prayer a priority in our lives.

Prayer Helps Us Maintain Focus

During times of trouble, it may be easy to lose focus and doubt God's goodness, or our place in the kingdom. As we observed in a previous chapter, trouble may tempt us to sin. In these times we must take steps to keep our focus on Christ. James exhorts those who are afflicted to pray (James 5:13). The Greek word translated afflicted in the KJV, and suffering in the ESV is a broad term that can refer to a range of human suffering. Trouble is an unpleasant reality of the human experience. Job lamented

> *"Man that is born of a woman is of few days, and full of trouble."*
> *Job 14:1*

Trouble could be the loss of a job, financial trouble, difficulties at home or work, a troubling medical diagnosis, the loss of a loved one, a wayward child, or a myriad of other issues we could name. In these times, we are instructed to seek God in prayer so that we might not lose focus. Our prayers in trying times often focus on rescue from the trouble we are facing, but we may not be delivered from our suffering in this life. Douglas Moo points out that,

> *"We might naturally think we would be encouraged to petition God to remove the trial. But James's concern when he deals with trials elsewhere (1:2-4, 12; 5:7-11) is to encourage believers to endure the suffering with the right spirit and with a divine perspective on the events in this world that affect us." Moo, 2000, 2021*

There is certainly nothing wrong with praying for deliverance as Paul did. But like Paul, we must trust in God's providential care over us. If God calls us to continue walking through suffering, prayer, and praise are valuable tools in keeping proper focus.

Prayer Provides Physical Healing

> *"Is any sick among you? let him call for the elders of the church; and let them pray over him, anointing him with oil in the name of the Lord: And the prayer of faith shall save the sick, and the Lord shall raise him up; and if he have committed sins, they shall be forgiven him." James 5:14-15*

Some fairly prominent false ideas are often put forward regarding this text, so it is necessary to briefly note these errors before explaining the truth James is writing. Many of our Catholic friends believe this passage is referring to extreme unction, also known as last rites. This cannot be the case since James does not call for prayers from a particular church leader. Furthermore, in James, it is assumed the individual being prayed over will receive healing whereas in extreme unction, the individual is dying.

Others view this passage to be a reference to the gift of healing in the New Testament Church. Many who hold this view are drawn to the healing crusades put on by so-called faith healers. It should be noted that James does not assume the power to heal is vested in any one person in the assembly nor does he call for a public display of healing. Instead, he instructs the sick individual to call for the church elders so they may pray over him or her. James may have a private prayer service in view. The scene James describes is far removed from the circus-like setting of healing crusades and ministries.

Finally, this text does not promise universal healing. The New Testament provides examples of individuals who did not receive healing. Paul instructed Timothy to drink a little wine to assist with his ailments (1 Timothy 5:23). Paul himself, as we have already discussed, suffered physical ailments (2 Corinthians 12:7). Paul left Trophimus at Miletum due to sickness, and Epaphroditus suffered so greatly Paul feared he would die (2 Timothy 4:20; Philippians 2:25-27). Absent in all these examples is a miraculous healing. It is evident that the gift of healing was not as prominent in the early church as some would have us believe, and it also seems the apostolic gifts in the church waned as the apostolic age came to a close.

In his commentary on James, Daniel Doriani recounts a

compelling and encouraging experience as a young elder in which a friend was healed of a viral heart infection. This friend called for the elders of the church, who then gathered to anoint him with oil and pray over Him. Doriani recalls,

> *"As soon as we began to pray, I had an overwhelming sense that God was, at that moment, healing my friend. My arms felt what I can only describe as bolts of fire pulsing through them. As I grasped my friend's shoulder, heat and energy burned in my hand. I felt that my one hand could lift all of his 230 pounds to the ceiling or push him through the floor if I wished." Doriani, 2007*

He kept the experience to himself because he was young and had never experienced anything of that nature before. A few days later he saw his friend at church and discovered that he had been healed! The two rejoiced together over the goodness of God and their faith was strengthened. None of us are promised a similar experience, but I share this to encourage all who read this to follow this Biblical precedent when appropriate. Not everyone is healed, but as this account so beautifully reminds us, many are. Regardless of what God ordains for us we can confidently follow God's Word and rest in His power.

James does not promise universal healing, but he does prescribe a process to follow when one in our assembly is sick. As we have already noted, the one who is sick is to take the initiative in calling the elders of the church to pray over them. Those who are called to pray over the sick person are to anoint them with oil in the name of the Lord. Verse fifteen promises that the prayer of faith will save the sick. The purpose and use of oil has been the subject of some debate, but it seems to be the case that oil should be used. In this instance, the oil is likely symbolic of the Holy Spirit and is a means of communicating that the individual being prayed over has been consecrated to the Lord.

James is clear "The prayer of faith shall save the sick". Faith is required in this prayer. Many wrongly define prayer as force and will assign lack of faith as the cause many are not healed. Faith, however, should not be viewed as a power or force we possess. Faith is trust in God. We rest in the sovereignty of God and humbly request that He answer our prayers. It is clear from the examples we have already given that lack of faith cannot always be assigned as the cause of why some are not healed. Nevertheless, we are instructed to pray in faith. James had already warned in chapter one that the prayer of the doubter will not be heard (James 1:6-7). Daniel Doriani warns us that,

> *"God will not heed a gathering of skeptics, who spin out a dead ritual." Doriani, 2007*

Though faith does not obligate God, we are required to pray in faith. Many have been healed in this way, but we should never make the mistake of assuming that the power to heal is vested in any single individual. God is able and we are not. Let us confidently call our God in the manner prescribed in this text, believing that our God can heal!

Prayer Provides Spiritual Restoration

At this point, we must discuss an unpopular reality presented in the text. James insists we must consider whether our sickness is caused by some sin we have not confessed. Notice what he writes.

> *"And the prayer of faith shall save the sick, and the Lord shall raise him up; and if he have committed sins, they shall be forgiven him.*
> *James 5:15*

This truth flies in the face of everything our culture tells us and goes against what is taught in many churches. To be clear, all suffering is ultimately caused by sin. We live in a world marred by sin, so suffering is an unpleasant reality in this life. This does not mean that all our suffering is caused directly by a sin we may have committed. We have discussed many in this study who suffered but were not guilty of any presumptuous or unconfessed sin. Nevertheless, we cannot be dismissive of the warning that sin may lead to suffering.

Many in our day indeed tend to over-spiritualize suffering. For these people, every sickness and trial is directly traceable to some sin we have committed or some devil we need deliverance from. This was also an issue during the earthly ministry of Christ. As the old saying goes, there is a ditch on both sides of the road. The ditch most evangelicals drive their proverbial car into is the ditch which insists suffering never stems from sin. But James is clear that the one who is suffering may be so due to their own sin.

Paul gave a similar warning in 1 Corinthians 11 in his

instructions regarding the Lord's supper. Those who partake of the Lord's supper in an unworthy fashion run the risk of judgment. This does not mean we are to be sin-free before we can partake of the Lord's table, for then we would never partake. To partake unworthily is to lightly regard the Lord's sacrifice. If the Spirit of God has revealed some sin to you, the proper response is to be grateful for grace, confess the sin, and receive the Lord's Supper. There is grace for those who humbly submit themselves to the Lordship of Christ.

James promises restoration for the one who has committed sins. He further instructs us in verse sixteen to confess our faults one to another and to pray for one another. This does not mean that we are to go to church at our next opportunity and air our spiritual dirty laundry for all to see, but it does mean that we are to seek the forgiveness of those we have sinned against. Perhaps you are reading this and the Holy Spirit has revealed a sin that you have been harboring and refusing to surrender. If you confess this sin you will find our Heavenly Father stands ready to forgive and cleanse you from all unrighteousness.

"Let the wicked forsake his way, and the unrighteous man his thoughts: and let him return unto the LORD, and he will have mercy upon him; and to our God, for he will abundantly pardon." Isaiah 55:7

Our God is slow to anger and abounding in mercy! Oh that God would give you the grace to cease from your anger, your running, and your unbelief and find rest in His loving arms!

I wish I could promise healing for all who seek it, but I cannot. I can however point you to One who is more than able. If He does not provide healing for you, He promises His grace is sufficient and His presence is always abiding. May God lead all of us to strengthen our prayer life so that in all things we seek our Lord in prayer. We can be sure that prayer is effective, but we must not judge the effectiveness of prayer by the physical results we measure. God is accomplishing His eternal plan in us. May God strengthen our faith in Him and through our trials grant us an abiding sense of His presence as we are being conformed into the image of Christ.

> *"Therefore, confess your sins to one another and pray for one another, that you may be healed. The prayer of a righteous person has great power as it is working." James 5:16*

8
No More Tears

"And I saw a new heaven and a new earth: for the first heaven and the first earth were passed away; and there was no more sea. And I John saw the holy city, new Jerusalem, coming down from God out of heaven, prepared as a bride adorned for her husband. And I heard a great voice out of heaven saying, Behold, the tabernacle of God is with men, and he will dwell with them, and they shall be his people, and God himself shall be with them, and be their God. And God shall wipe away all tears from their eyes; and there shall be no more death, neither sorrow, nor crying, neither shall there be any more pain: for the former things are passed away." Revelation 21:1-4

The day my mother died is indelibly etched into my mind. I suspect the vividness of that memory will never fade. I was twenty-six and living in St. Louis when I received word she would no longer be in this world. My wife and I packed up the kids and rushed home to North Carolina to spend whatever precious moments we could with the godliest woman I have ever known. That morning, I woke early, sat by her bedside, and gently took her hand in mine. It felt cold-just as the hospice nurse had said it would. I stayed for a bit longer and then sat down in the adjacent room next to my wife. I whispered, "Her hands are cold." My precious wife knew what that meant, so we just sat there, our minds swirling. A few hours later my wife and I, along with my siblings, their spouses, and my dad, sat around her bedside and told her we loved her. Just moments after the last one breathed, "I love you", she was gone At that moment, I understood what it was like for sorrow and hope to mingle. My dad, through tears, prayed aloud, "O Father! We know you do all things well."

In the days that followed, I was simply inconsolable. My wife, Debbie, wanted to help and her presence was a great comfort, but she could not speak peace to my soul the way the Savior did as I prayed while walking down my dad's gravel road. My prayer was simply, "Lord, I can't." At her funeral, I had the privilege of leading the congregation in the hymn "What A Day That Will Be" and I don't think a church ever sounded as lovely as it did that day. The passing of my mother brought great sorrow and even now tears blur the screen as I type. But one day, our Lord will wipe every tear away. For now, sorrow is mingled with hope, but one day sorrow will fade into distant memory.

Revelation 21 describes a glorious scene in which the Apostle John sees the future new heaven and earth. He describes the passing away of the first heaven and earth and even declares there will be no more sea. This is a bit puzzling for sure but is probably a symbolic way of describing a world where all trouble and sorrow are removed. This language reflects the fear ancient people had of the sea. The ocean was not a vacation spot. It represented a dangerous way to earn a livelihood and travel. The storms arising from the ocean were often devastating.

The promise of Revelation represents the promise of joy and peace for God's people. John describes a future in which the old things are all passed away. The new heaven and earth are described primarily by what is absent. Robert Mounce notes,

> *"Eternal blessedness is couched in negation because the new and glorious order is more easily pictured in terms of what it replaces then by an attempt to describe what is largely inconceivable in our present state." Mounce, 1977*

The future blessed state of the believer has been the subject of many books, songs, and sermons. Too often our focus is on the physical beauty of Heaven rather than the King who sits on the throne and is the light of the city. One such song titled "Mansion Over the Hilltop" is based on John 14:2 and highlights the bright, beautiful, and personal mansion awaiting the faithful. This song reflects a worldly and covetous spirit embraced by many believers and is based on a misunderstanding of the text. The word translated 'mansions' by the KJV refers simply to a place of dwelling. Furthermore, the word mansion did not carry the same meaning in 1611 that it does in present times. According to Webster's 1828 dictionary, the word mansion means

> *"Any place of residence; a house; a habitation." Webster, 1967*

We should note here that in John 14 our Lord is assuring His disciples that they will one day dwell with Him forever, and the langue does not warrant a belief that all Christians will have their own personal mansion. This is not intended to burst any bubbles, but to highlight our tendency to focus on materialism even when reflecting on the future state.

This future blessedness appeals to us because our current existence is marred by suffering which causes us to fix our gaze Heavenward (Romans 8:22). But more than this, there is in us something that forces us to recognize there is more to life than what we see. Soloman stated that God has placed eternity into our hearts (Ecclesiastes 3:11). There is in every man an awareness of God and the eternal state of the human soul.

Revelation 21 then represents in part the culmination of the unfolding drama of redemption recorded in Scripture. Though we don't have time for a detailed recounting of this drama, we will fly over, as it were, at 30,000 feet. May the Lord use these words to give you an appreciation of Christ's redemptive work and cause you to look even more intently to our blessed hope and glorious appearance of our great God and Savior Jesus Christ (Titus 2:13).

The Kingdom Promised

It is difficult to imagine the original beauty of the garden created by God. Even the most beautiful places we visit now are marred by the curse of sin. No place on earth matches the perfection of the Garden of Eden. God declared throughout the creation account that it was very good. Amid this beautiful garden, God placed man whom He created in His own image (Genesis 1:26) in the garden to rule over it.

Here, man was given everything. He lacked nothing, lived in perfect happiness, enjoyed the presence of God, and fulfilled God's purpose on earth. Jeffrey Johnson described God's purpose for the garden in his scholarly work, "The Kingdom of God." Johnson explains,

> *"The Kingdom of man was also to be the Kingdom of God. Although the children of the Kingdom were the sons of men, the sons of men were created to be the sons of God. God made man in his own image. God made man upright. God gave man a dominion that was declared good. Therefore, the perfection of heaven was to be the perfection upon earth, for the earth was to mirror heaven as man was to mirror God."*
> *Johnson, 2016*

Upon creating man, God placed him in the garden, gave him dominion over creation, tasked him with maintaining the garden, and instructed him to be fruitful and multiply in the earth (Genesis 1:27-30; 2:15). In this paradise man was given a single prohibition. He was not to eat of the tree of the knowledge of good and evil.

> *"But of the tree of the knowledge of good and evil, thou shalt not eat of it: for in the day that thou eatest thereof thou shalt surely die." Genesis 2:17*

Adam was in a covenant of works. So long as he lived in the garden and obeyed God, he would live in happiness eternally in the blessed state in which he was created. If He disobeyed God, death was promised. The blessedness of

Adam rested on his decision. Skeptics argue that God was somehow unfair by placing a tree in the garden which man should not partake of, but such a charge is absurd. If I were to allow one or all of my children to live in my house, give them access to all I have in the house, and ask that they leave one small table by my bed alone, no rational person would call me unkind or unfair. The skeptic reveals more than he wishes to in his objections.

Man fell from this original state and suffered the just consequences of sin. The immediate consequences of Adam's sin were the guilt associated with sin displayed by the desire to hide from God, the righteous judgment of God, and removal from the garden of Eden. The fall of man also resulted in the ground being cursed. His life would now be marked by toil and labor to subsist on this earth. The woman was cursed with pain in childbearing. Their sin led to a loss of the state of holiness in which they were created. Adam's immortality was contingent upon his obedience to God, so the first sin led to the loss of immortality. Both would die physically, but their spiritual death and separation from God was immediate (Genesis 3). We too fell with Adam's sin. In Adam, we all sin and in Adam, we all die.

> *"Wherefore, as by one man sin entered into the world, and death by sin; and so, death passed upon all men, for that all have sinned."*
> *Romans 5:12*

Though this creature from the dust defied the living and

true God, mercy was shown. God graciously clothed Adam and Eve and even promised a future redeemer who would defeat the serpent and remove the curse (Genesis 3:15). Suffering in this present world is due to the fact that we are sinful and live in a fallen world.

The Gospel Promise

The gospel promise was that God would redeem a people for His Son. Jeffery Johson observes,

> *"The gospel came because Christ was determined to have a Kingdom and he would not be refused the inheritance of his promised people."*
> *Johnson, 2016*

Hope was not lost. God would raise a kingdom. Genesis 3:15 represents the first promise of the gospel and it did not take long for the kingdom to suffer opposition. Cain killed brother Abel, and such has been the nature of the kingdom since the first promise (Genesis 4). When Jesus met the disciples on the road to Emmaus, He explained the Christocentric nature of the Scriptures. Luke writes,

> *"And beginning at Moses and all the prophets, he expounded unto them in all the scriptures the things concerning himself." Luke 24:27*

All of Scripture points to the reign of Christ. That's what we mean when we speak of His kingdom. We are speaking of the reign of God through His Son Jesus. God called Abram and promised that through him the Messiah would come, and all nations would be blessed (Genesis 15,17,22). God rescued Israel from Egypt and on Mt. Sainai God established the Mosaic Covenant. Later in her history, the people of Israel would demand a king. Israel was called to fulfill the role of Adam and to typify Christ, but where Adam failed Israel failed also. Abraham, Moses, the Aaronic priesthood, and the Davidic Kingdom failed to bring about the kingdom, so the people of God would have to wait.

> *"How long wilt thou forget me, O LORD? forever? How long wilt thou hide thy face from me? How long shall I take counsel in my soul, having sorrow in my heart daily? How long shall mine enemy be exalted over me? Consider and hear me, O LORD my God: lighten mine eyes, lest I sleep the sleep of death; Lest mine enemy say, I have prevailed against him; and those that trouble me rejoice when I am moved. But I have trusted in thy mercy; my heart shall rejoice in thy salvation. I will sing unto the LORD, because he hath dealt bountifully with me." Psalm 13:1-6*

The Kingdom Inaugurated

In him was life; and the life was the light of men. And the light shineth in darkness; and the darkness comprehended it not. John 1:4-5

The relative darkness represented in the Old Testament was dispelled by the announcement of the birth of John the Baptist and the Messiah (Luke 1). The birth of the King was celebrated by the angelic host who proclaimed,

"For unto you is born this day in the city of David a Saviour, which is Christ the Lord." Luke 2:11

Johnson points out that,

"The gospel which was only a flicker in the Old Testament, was about to be set ablaze… the New Testament opens with the Kingdom of God at hand because it opens with the glorious announcement of the birth of the king of Israel." Johnson, 2016

John the Baptist leaped in the mother's womb at the very presence of Jesus who was still in the womb of His mother (Luke 1:41). Simeon rejoiced when He saw the Christ child at the temple.

"Then took he him up in his arms, and blessed God, and said, Lord, now lettest thou thy servant depart in peace, according to thy word: For mine eyes have seen thy salvation, Which thou hast prepared before the face of all people; A light to lighten the Gentiles, and the glory of thy people Israel." Luke 2:28-32

The King had been born and He was the light of the world. The forces of darkness would not give up. Herod tried to kill Christ, but the Father protected His son in Egypt until it was safe for Him to return (Matthew 2:15; Hosea 11:1). John the Baptist was born to be the forerunner of the Messiah. The angel Gabriel proclaimed regarding John,

> *"And he shall go before him in the spirit and power of Elias, to turn the hearts of the fathers to the children, and the disobedient to the wisdom of the just; to make ready a people prepared for the Lord."*
> Luke 1:17

John, just as the angel promised, came out of the wilderness and began to proclaim the kingdom of God. He implored the people to repent and be baptized in preparation for the Messiah. John's preaching was a proclamation of the Kingdom.

> *"In those days came John the Baptist, preaching in the wilderness of Judaea, And saying, Repent ye: for the kingdom of heaven is at hand. For this is he that was spoken of by the prophet Esaias, saying, "The voice of one crying in the wilderness, Prepare ye the way of the Lord, make his paths straight."* Mathew 3:1-3; Isaiah 40:3

When John saw Jesus approaching the river Jordan he called on all present to look to the lamb of God who alone would save the world from sin (John 1:36).

> *"Now after that John was put in prison, Jesus came into Galilee, preaching the gospel of the kingdom of God, And saying, The time is fulfilled, and the kingdom of God is at hand: repent ye, and believe the gospel."* Mark 1:14-15

When Jesus began His ministry, He proclaimed the kingdom. His sermons were about the kingdom. His teaching explained what the kingdom was like, and His miracles demonstrated the power of the kingdom and gave authentication to His claims. His parables explained the nature of the kingdom to His disciples. These parables served to enlighten the disciples and keep the reprobate in darkness (Matthew 13:11). The central focus of the ministry of Christ was the kingdom. Hans Wunch in his book, "Proclaiming The Kingdom of God," points out that

"Jesus talked more about the Kingdom of God than any other subject contained in the gospels. It is clear that the Kingdom of God is central and is central to Christ's message." Wunch, 2022

When Jesus cast out demons, he was proclaiming His kingdom. He was giving notice that He was stepping into the domain of darkness and taking rule. Jesus declared, But if I cast out devils by the Spirit of God, then the kingdom of God is come unto you. Or else how can one enter into a strong man's house, and spoil his goods, except he first bind the strong man? and then he will spoil his house (Matthew 12:28-29). Jesus is the king who sets the captives free and makes all things new.

Jesus through His life, death, and ascension inaugurated the kingdom of God. Adam failed to keep the law of God as did Abraham, Moses, David, and all Israel. No one could satisfy the demands of the law. No one could bring about the kingdom of God. But, what Adam could not do, Jesus did. What Moses could not do, Christ did. What Israel failed to do, Jesus did. Jesus satisfied the demands of the law (Matthew 3:13-16). He also suffered the curse of the law

(Galatians 3:13). As the last Adam, Jesus regained all that Adam lost (1 Corinthians 15:45-49; Romans 5:12-14).

The redeemer promised in Genesis 3:15 would crush the head of the serpent. Through His work on the cross, Christ satisfied the wrath of God, purchased redemption for His people, and reconciled us to the Father. (Galatians 2:20, Romans 5:1-8, Hebrews 1:3) Jesus through death defeated Satan and death. The author of Hebrews reminds us,

> *"Forasmuch then as the children are partakers of flesh and blood, he also himself likewise took part of the same; that through death he might destroy him that had the power of death, that is, the devil; And deliver them who through fear of death were all their lifetime subject to bondage."* Hebrews 2:14-15

Christ rose again and is now seated at the right of the Father interceding for us. (Romans 8:34; 1 John 2:1)

The Kingdom Consummated

> *"Then cometh the end, when he shall have delivered up the Kingdom to God, even the father; When he shall have put down all rule and all authority and power, for he must reign, till he hath put all enemies under his feet."* 1 Corinthians 15:24-25

It is finished! Far from being a cry of defeat, this was a victor's shout. Christ had, as promised in Genesis 3:15, crushed the head of the serpent. Jesus' death and resurrection dealt a mortal blow to Satan. He no longer would be able to hold the saints accountable for the debt accumulated by sin. Jesus had paid the debt and ransomed His people. The ruler of darkness had been cast out. The Savior proclaimed in John 12:31-33,

"Now is the judgment of this world: now shall the prince of this world be cast out. And I, if I be lifted up from the earth, will draw all men unto me. This said he, signifying what death he should die."

Remember earlier when we quoted Matthew 12: 28-29? In that passage, Jesus proclaimed the kingdom by showing He had power over darkness. He had entered the strong man's house and proved Himself to be mightier. Satan is often called the prince of this world, but Christ was disarming him and casting him out. When Jesus died and rose again, he cast Satan out and bound him so that he could no longer deceive the nations. Revelation 20:1-3 proclaims,

"And I saw an Angel come down from heaven, having the key of the bottomless pit and a great chain in his hand. And he laid hold on the dragon, that old serpent, which is the devil, and Satan, and bound him 1000 years, and cast him into the bottomless pit, and shut him up, and set a seal upon him that he should deceive the nations no more, till the 1000 years should be fulfilled: and after that he must be loosed a little season."

How could it be that Satan is bound if the world is so wicked and Satan still seems so active? The binding of Satan as described in the above passage is designed to prevent him from continuing to deceive the nations. Jeffrey

Johnson observes,

> "Before the cross, the kingdoms of this world were under the control of the Prince of Darkness. Moreover, in the Old Testament dispensation, international missions were basically non-existent. God worked with a small remnant out of a tiny nation, Israel, and left the rest of the nations and people groups of the world to themselves. Thus, the nations of the world groped around in darkness as they willingly took their marching orders from the prince of the power of the air period."
> Johnson, 2016

That all changed after the cross! The nations would no longer be deceived, they were no longer Satan's domain. Christ would proclaim to His disciples that all authority had been given to Him; on that basis, He sent them all over the globe to make disciples. The gospel exploded across the earth and the Kingdom expanded. Even some 2000 years later, the gospel of the kingdom continues to be proclaimed and Christ is king.

The kingdom of God is a present reality, and we enjoy the benefits of it now. Christ has satisfied the curse of the law, the power of sin over us is broken, and death has been defeated. We now rest in the finished work of Christ. Christ is the substance of which the Old Testament shadows pointed. There is an already aspect of the kingdom of God, but we still wait for the consummation of all things. A helpful phrase to help in understanding the Kingdom and our eschatological hope is "already and net yet." There are benefits of the kingdom that are present and there are some not yet present. This is the already, not yet aspect of the kingdom. The curse of the law has been satisfied, but the whole creation still groans under sin (Romans 8:22). The power of sin is broken, but we still sin (Romans 7). Death has been defeated, but we still die. We rest in Christ, but we still long for an eternal rest free from sin, worry, and discouragement. Satan has been defeated, but it is self-evident that he is still active. His head has been crushed but as Revelation 12:17 indicates, he still makes war with the saints. We still await the day when our Savior will make all things new.

The already, not yet aspect of the kingdom is where prosperity teachers, and in my view, the entire continuationist movement falters. A continuationist believes the apostolic gifts have ceased. Conversely, a cessationist believes the gifts have ceased. There are many errors in the prosperity movement, but this is a glaring one. Daniel Kolenda, president of Christ For All Nations, and successor to Reinhardt Bonnke writes,

"When the kingdom comes, that means God's will is being done. "Heal the sick, cleanse the lepers, raise the dead" ... Yes, part of our job is raising the dead. Now, I've seen three people come back from the dead. I've prayed for a lot more than three. But I can tell you one thing, there is power in the gospel even to reverse death. I think that "raise the dead" is in this Commission because of the extreme quality of death. I think what Jesus is trying to tell us is that there is nothing that is beyond the reach of the power of the gospel. Even death itself has to bow." Kolenda, 2024

I have no reason to doubt Daniel Kolenda's sincerity, but this is a grievous error. His error is due largely to a fundamental misunderstanding of the kingdom. Scripture tells us the final enemy to be defeated is death, but we know death is still a present reality. (1 Corinthians 15:26). Similarly, we still sin, though as God's people we hate it. If the kingdom was fully consummated, we would be free from the very presence of sin. The Apostle John reminds us of a future day when all things will be made new. John writes,

"And God shall wipe away all tears from their eyes; and there shall be no more death, neither sorrow, nor crying, neither shall there be any more pain: for the former things are passed away." Revelation 21:4

Tears, death, sorrow, and pain will be removed on that blessed day. Given this glorious promise and the nature of our current reality, we must conclude that we still await the consummation of His kingdom. What a glorious day it will be when our Lord makes all things new! On that day, He will, as a loving Father, take away all our pain and sorrow. Authors Joel Beeke and Paul Smalley note,

"The bride of the Lord has suffered great wounds in body and spirit, bitter consequences of her own sins and the sins of her tempters and oppressors. Heaven is a place of healing, where God will apply his comfort so deeply that all sorrow will disappear forever. In the kingdom of God, believers will know by experience that "they that sow in tears reap and joy Psalm 126:5." Smalley, 2024

Never again will a mother bury her small child. Never again will we gather around loved ones as they breathe their final breath. The sorrow and disease we will struggle with here will be little more than a distant memory. No longer will we fight with sin. Satan will no longer war against the Church for he will be destroyed forever. We will no longer mourn over the treatment of Christians around the world. Wicked rulers will no longer hold sway over helpless citizens for Christ will exact His vengeance on all His enemies. All tears are wiped away. Beeke and Smalley again comment,

"The image is one of God's tender and compassionate touch, as a father or mother would wipe tears off the face of a beloved child while soothing pain and quieting fear." Smalley, 2024

Best of all, we will dwell in the presence of our dear Savior for eternity. He will be the light of that city, and we will join the Heavenly anthem as the saints of all the ages along with the saints, sing "Worthy is the lamb." We will with one voice make the Celestial City ring with the shouts of Holy, Holy, Holy, is the Lord God Almighty. Saint don't lose heart; we will soon behold the face of our Loving Savior, and it will be worth it all.

He which testifieth these things sayeth, surely, I come quickly. Amen. Even so, come, Lord Jesus. The grace of our Lord Jesus Christ be with you all. Amen. Revelation 22:20-21

Bibliography

Barger, D. (2022, August 9). Pillars Of Truth For Baptist Churches. Knightstown, Indiana: Particular Baptist Heritage Books. Retrieved from relight.app: https://relight.app/

Beeke, M. (2007). The Law of Kindness . Grand Rapids, Michigan : Reformation Heritage Books.

Bishop, J. (2016, June 27). Bishop's Encyclopedia of Religion, Society and Philosophy. Retrieved from jamesbishopblog.com: https://jamesbishopblog.com/2016/06/27/answering-the-epicurus-dilemma/

Brown, J. (1819). A Compendious View of Natural and Revealed Religion . Philidelphia : David Hogan.

Charles Hodge, D. (1877). Systematic Theology Volume II. New York : Scribner, Armstrong, and CO.

Charnock, S. (2024). Calvinism's Answer To The Problem Of Evil. West Linn, OR: Monergism Books.

Clark, G. H. (1961, 20004). God And Evil The problem Solved. Unicoi, Tennesee : The Trinity Foundation.

Doriani, D. M. (2007). Reformed Expository Commentary. Phillipsburg, New Jersy : P&R Publishing .

Elliot, E. (2019). Suffering Is Never For Nothing . Nasheville, Tennesee : B&H Publishing Group.

Hodge, C. (1857,2023). 1&2 Corinthians . East Peoria, Illinois : Banner of Truth Trust.

Johnson, J. D. (2016). The Kingdom Of God. A Baptist Expression of Covenant & Biblical Theology. Conway, Arkansas: Free Grace Press .

Jr, C. A. (1999). Total Life Prosperity . Nasheville, Tennesee: Thomas Nelson .

Kolenda, D. (2024, August 17). As You Go, Preach. Retrieved from Christ For All Nations : www.cfan.eu

Lewis, C. (1952). Mere Christianity. London : Geoffry Bles.

Masters, P. (1998, 2013). The Healing Epedemic . London, England : The Wakeman Trust.

Moo, D. (2000, 2021). The Letter of James . Grand Rapids, Michigan : Wm. B. Eerdmans Publishing Co.

Mounce, R. H. (1977). The Book of Revelation . Grand Rapids, Michigan: Wm. B. Eerdmans Publishing Co. .

Myers, R. (2020, April 1st). e-Sword 12.2.0. Franklin, Tenessee, USA.

Ogden, G. (2007). Discipleship Esserntials . Downers Grave, Illinois : InterVarsity Press.

Phillips, J. (1977,1988). Exploring Hebrews. Neptune, New Jersey : Loizeaux Brothers .

Pink, A. (1949). The Sovereignty of God.

Press, F. (2017). The 1689 Baptist Confession of Faith in Modern Englsih. Cape Coral, Florida : Founders Press .

Pringle, J. C. (2010). Commentaries on the Epistles of Pasul the Apostle to the Corinthians . Bellingham, WA, USA.

R. L. Dabney, D. L. (1878). Systematic And Polemic Theology . St. Louis : Presbyterian Publishing Company of St. Louis .

Smalley, J. R. (2024). Reformed Systematic Theology: Church and Last Things. Wheaton, Illinois: Crossway.

Smith, D. W. (2020). Ore From The Puritan's Mine. Grand Rapids Michigan : Reformation Heritage Books.

SOBOLIK, C. P. (2014, December 5). Suffering: For God's Glory and Your Good. Retrieved from The Gospel Coalition : https://www.thegospelcoalition.org/article/suffering-for-gods-glory-and-your-good/

Sproul, R. (2009). John . Sanford, Florida: Reformation Trust Publishing.

Storms, S. (2008, August 1). Paul's Thorn in The Flesh . Retrieved from Enjoying God : Samstorms.org

Webster, N. (1967). American Dictionary Of The Englsih language . San Fansisco, California : Foundation for American Christian Education.

Wilfred Jackson, H. L. (Director). (1950). Cinderellla [Motion Picture].

William G.T. Shedd, D. (1888). Dogmatic Theology. New York : Charles Scribner's Sons .

Woodbridge, D. W. (2017). Health, Wealth, and Prosperity: How the Prosperity Gospel Overshaddows the Gospel of Christ. Grand Rapids, MI: Kregal Publications .

Wunch, H. (2022). Proclaiming the Kingdom of God. Albany, Georgia : Self Published.

About the Author

John Kuykendall is the pastor of Pilgrim's Rest Baptist Church in Hillsboro, Missouri. Originally from Hendersonville, North Carolina, he has been married to his high school sweetheart, Debbie, for 26 years. They have three wonderful children. John is a 1998 graduate of Tabernacle Baptist Bible College and is currently pursuing a Master of Christian Studies through Forge Theological Seminary.

John is grateful for every reader who takes the time to engage with this book. His prayer is that it will be an encouragement to those who read it and that, above all, Christ will be glorified.

He can be contacted through the website of Pilgrim's Rest Baptist Church at
https://www.pilgrimsrestbaptist.church/

www.ingramcontent.com/pod-product-compliance
Lightning Source LLC
Chambersburg PA
CBHW050521100526
44581CB00002B/57